Quick Tips

Visual®

by Kate Shoup

1807
WILEY
2007

Wiley Publishing, Inc.

# iPhone™ VISUAL™ Quick Tips

Published by
Wiley Publishing, Inc.
10475 Crosspoint Boulevard
Indianapolis, IN 46256

Published simultaneously in Canada

Copyright © 2008 by Wiley Publishing, Inc.,
Indianapolis, Indiana

Library of Congress Control Number: 2007940112

ISBN: 978-0-470-17371-8

Manufactured in the United States of America

10 9 8 7 6 5 4 3 2 1

## Trademark Acknowledgments

## Contact Us

For general information on our other products and
services contact our Customer Care Department within
the U.S. at 800-762-2974, outside the U.S. at
317-572-3993, or fax 317-572-4002.

For technical support please visit
www.wiley.com/techsupport.

WILEY

Wiley Publishing, Inc.

**Sales**

Contact Wiley
at (800) 762-2974 or
fax (317) 572-4002.

# Praise for Visual Books

"I have to praise you and your company on the fine products you turn out. I have twelve Visual books in my house. They were instrumental in helping me pass a difficult computer course. Thank you for creating books that are easy to follow. Keep turning out those quality books."

Gordon Justin (Brielle, NJ)

"What fantastic teaching books you have produced! Congratulations to you and your staff. You deserve the Nobel prize in Education. Thanks for helping me understand computers."

Bruno Tonon (Melbourne, Australia)

"A Picture Is Worth A Thousand Words! If your learning method is by observing or hands-on training, this is the book for you!"

Lorri Pegan-Durastante (Wickliffe, OH)

"Over time, I have bought a number of your 'Read Less - Learn More' books. For me, they are THE way to learn anything easily. I learn easiest using your method of teaching."

José A. Mazón (Cuba, NY)

"You've got a fan for life!! Thanks so much!!"

Kevin P. Quinn (Oakland, CA)

"I have several books from the Visual series and have always found them to be valuable resources."

Stephen P. Miller (Ballston Spa, NY)

"I have several of your Visual books and they are the best I have ever used."

Stanley Clark (Crawfordville, FL)

"Like a lot of other people, I understand things best when I see them visually. Your books really make learning easy and life more fun."

John T. Frey (Cadillac, MI)

"I have quite a few of your Visual books and have been very pleased with all of them. I love the way the lessons are presented!"

Mary Jane Newman (Yorba Linda, CA)

"Thank you, thank you, thank you...for making it so easy for me to break into this high-tech world."

Gay O'Donnell (Calgary, Alberta,Canada)

"I write to extend my thanks and appreciation for your books. They are clear, easy to follow, and straight to the point. Keep up the good work! I bought several of your books and they are just right! No regrets! I will always buy your books because they are the best."

Seward Kollie (Dakar, Senegal)

"I would like to take this time to thank you and your company for producing great and easy-to-learn products. I bought two of your books from a local bookstore, and it was the best investment I've ever made! Thank you for thinking of us ordinary people."

Jeff Eastman (West Des Moines, IA)

"Compliments to the chef!! Your books are extraordinary! Or, simply put, extra-ordinary, meaning way above the rest! THANKYOU THANKYOU THANKYOU! I buy them for friends, family, and colleagues."

Christine J. Manfrin (Castle Rock, CO)

# Credits

**Acquisitions Editor**
Jody Lefevere

**Copy Editor**
Marylouise Wiack

**Editorial Manager**
Robyn Siesky

**Business Manager**
Amy Knies

**Manufacturing**
Allan Conley
Linda Cook
Paul Gilchrist
Jennifer Guynn

**Book Design**
Kathie S. Rickard

**Production Coordinator**
Lynsey Osborn

**Layout**
Carrie A. Cesavice
Andrea Hornberger
Stephanie D. Jumper
Amanda Spagnuolo

**Screen Artist**
Jill A. Proll

**Cover Design**
Anthony Bunyan

**Proofreader**
Broccoli Information Management

**Quality Control**
Laura Albert

**Indexer**
Slivoskey Indexing Services

**Vice President and Executive Group Publisher**
Richard Swadley

**Vice President Publisher**
Barry Pruett

**Composition Director**
Debbie Stailey

**Wiley Bicentennial Logo**
Richard J. Pacifico

# How To Use This Book

*iPhone VISUAL Quick Tips* includes more than 90 tasks that reveal cool secrets, teach timesaving tricks, and explain great tips guaranteed to make you more productive with using your new iPhone. The easy-to-use layout lets you work through all the tasks from beginning to end or jump in at random.

## Who Is This Book For?

If you want to know the basics about using your iPhone, or if you want to learn shortcuts, tricks, and tips that let you work smarter and faster, this book is for you. And because you learn more easily when someone *shows* you how, this is the book for you.

## Conventions Used In This Book

### ❶ Introduction
The introduction is designed to get you up to speed on the topic at hand.

### ❷ Steps
This book uses step-by-step instructions to guide you easily through each task. Numbered callouts on every screen shot show you exactly how to perform each task, step by step.

### ❸ Tips
Practical tips provide insights to save you time and trouble, caution you about hazards to avoid, and reveal how to do things with iPhone that you never thought possible!

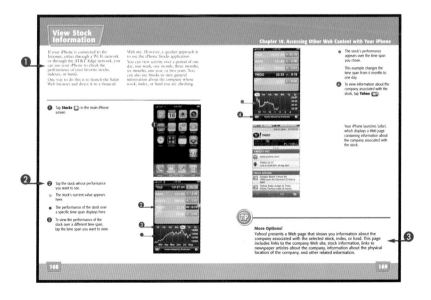

# Table of Contents

**Getting Started with Your iPhone**

**Personalizing Your iPhone**

**Using Your iPhone as a PDA**

### chapter 4  Using Your iPhone as a Mobile Phone

### chapter 5  Sending and Receiving E-Mail and Text Messages with Your iPhone

chapter **6** Enjoying Audio Content on Your iPhone

chapter **7** **Enjoying Video Content on Your iPhone**

chapter 8 — Using Your iPhone to Take and Share Photos

chapter 9 — Surfing the Web with Your iPhone

# Getting Started with Your iPhone

You can use your iPhone to perform many tasks, such as sending and retrieving e-mail messages, placing and receiving phone calls, and surfing the Internet. You can also check the weather, track stocks, calculate a restaurant tip, enjoy your favorite songs and videos, and take photographs.

Before you can use your iPhone, you must first set it up by downloading and installing iTunes on your computer. You use iTunes to transfer media files, photos, contacts, calendar entries, and other content from your computer to your iPhone. You must also set up your AT&T wireless account for your iPhone, associate your iPhone with your Apple ID, establish sync preferences, and set up your voicemail. This chapter shows you how to do all of this, as well as how to access iTunes' help feature.

# Quick Tips

# Download iTunes to a PC

You can use iTunes to manage and play music and other media content on your computer. Your iPhone is designed to work in conjunction with iTunes. You can sync your iPhone with iTunes in order to transfer media content, as well as photos, contacts, and calendar entries, from your computer to your iPhone.

In order to use iTunes with your iPhone, you must first download and install the iTunes program. The download and installation operations involve stepping through a series of screens in order to specify your preferences. For example, you can specify where the iTunes program file should be saved on your computer, and whether you want to receive newsletters from Apple.

① Type **www.apple.com/itunes/download** in your Web browser and then press **Enter**.

The Download iTunes page opens.

● Your operating system appears here.

● You can click here to receive the New Music Tuesday newsletter from Apple ( changes to ).

● You can click here to receive Apple news and software updates ( changes to ).

② Type your e-mail address.

③ Click **Download iTunes Free**.

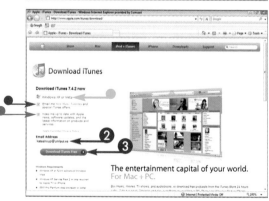

A Security Warning appears, asking whether you want to run or save the iTunes Setup file.

④ Click **Run**.

Your computer downloads the iTunes Installer program.

Another Security Warning appears, asking if you want to run iTunes.

⑤ Click **Run**.

**Attention!**

Apple occasionally updates its iTunes software to resolve bugs and add new features. To check whether you have the most recent version of the software, open the iTunes Help menu and choose **Check for Updates**. iTunes checks to see whether you have the most current version; if not, it guides you through the update process. You must be online to check for updates.

After you download iTunes to your computer, you can use it to manage and play media content on your computer. This includes music, movies, TV shows, audio and video podcasts, audio books, and Internet radio stations. It allows you to access the iTunes Store, where you can purchase content. You can also use iTunes to create playlists of your favorite songs and videos.

If you choose to place a shortcut to iTunes on your Windows desktop, you can launch the program by double-clicking the shortcut. Alternatively, you can launch iTunes by clicking the Start button, clicking All Programs, clicking the iTunes folder, and clicking iTunes.

The Welcome to the iTunes Installer dialog box appears.

**6** Click **Next** to continue.

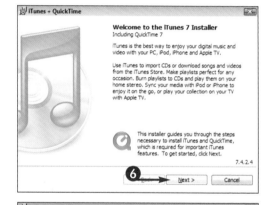

The Apple license agreement appears for iTunes.

**7** Click **I accept the terms in the license agreement** (⊙ changes to ⦿).

**8** Click **Next**.

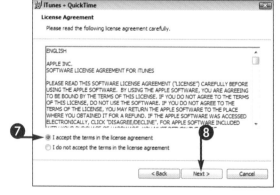

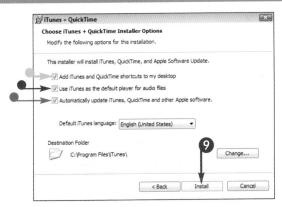

The Choose iTunes + QuickTime Installer Options screen appears.

● Click **Add iTunes and QuickTime shortcuts to my desktop** to install the iTunes and QuickTime desktop shortcuts (☐ changes to ☑).

● Click **Use iTunes as the default player for audio files** to select iTunes as your default audio player (☐ changes to ☑).

● Click **Automatically Update iTunes** to automate the update process (☐ changes to ☑).

⑨ Click **Install**.

The Congratulations screen appears.

⑩ Click **Finish**.

iTunes downloads to your PC.

### Important!

If you decide not to make iTunes the default player for these types of content now, but later change your mind, you can change the default player settings. Open the Edit menu in iTunes and choose **Preferences**. In the dialog box that appears, click the **Advanced** tab, click **General**, and then select the **Use iTunes as the default player for audio files** check box.

# Download iTunes to a Mac

The main purpose of iTunes is to enable you to manage and enjoy music and other media content on your computer, such as movies, TV episodes, audio books, and podcasts. However, you can also use iTunes to sync your iPhone with your computer. *Syncing* transfers media content, as well as photos, contacts, calendar entries, and other content, from your computer to your iPhone.

Luckily for Mac users, Apple includes iTunes, as well as QuickTime, in every version of Mac OS X it distributes. If you have not used iTunes, your copy may not be the latest version. Apple updates iTunes frequently to ensure compatibility with new hardware such as the iPhone. Fortunately, the updating process is simple.

① Click .

② Click **Software Update**.

The Software Update dialog box appears, informing you of any new versions of software installed on your Mac.

③ Click **iTunes** ( changes to ).

④ Click **Install**.

**Note:** *In order to install a new version of iTunes, Software Update requires you to type an Administrator password and accept the terms of a software license agreement.*

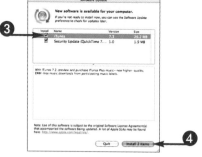

Software Update downloads and installs the new version of iTunes.

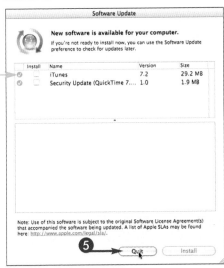

● Software Update displays an Import Complete icon (🗹) to indicate the download process is complete.

❺ Click **Quit** to close the dialog box.

iTunes is made available on your Mac.

### Attention!

To launch iTunes, click the **iTunes** icon in the Dock. The first time you do this, iTunes displays the Apple license agreement; click **Accept**. You are then asked a series of questions in order to set your preferences; simply follow the onscreen prompts. When setup is complete, the iTunes window appears.

# Configure Your iPhone for Use

After you download and launch the latest version of iTunes, you must configure your iPhone for use. To begin, you must connect your iPhone to your computer using the cable that came with your iPhone. iTunes then displays a special Welcome screen that outlines the steps you must take in order to use your iPhone.

The first step is to activate your iPhone with AT&T, specifying whether you are a new or existing customer and whether you want to port your existing mobile number to your iPhone. You must also select the wireless plan you want to use. After you do this, you can sync your iPhone with iTunes to copy your contacts, photos, and media to the iPhone.

① Connect your iPhone to your computer.

The Welcome to Your New iPhone screen appears.

② Click **Continue**.

The Are You a New or Existing AT&T (Cingular) Wireless Customer? screen appears.

③ Click **Activate one iPhone now** (○ changes to ◉).

④ Click **Continue**.

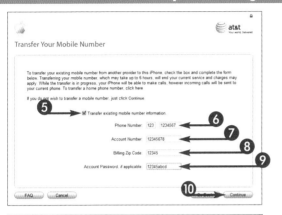

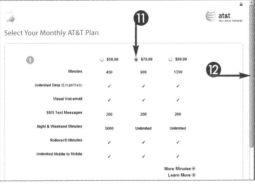

The Transfer Your Mobile Number screen appears.

**⑤** Click **Transfer existing mobile number information** (☐ changes to ☑).

**⑥** Type the phone number you want to transfer to your iPhone.

**⑦** Type the account number for your current wireless plan.

**⑧** Type the Zip Code of your billing address.

**⑨** Type the account password for your current wireless plan.

**⑩** Click **Continue**.

AT&T verifies the account information for the mobile number you want to transfer, and the Select Your Monthly AT&T Plan screen appears.

**⑪** Click the plan you want to purchase (◯ changes to ◉).

**⑫** Drag the scroll bar downward.

### Attention!

This section contains the specific steps for setting up an iPhone where the user is a new AT&T wireless customer transferring an existing number to a single iPhone. If you are an existing customer, acquiring a new number, or activating multiple phones, the steps will differ slightly; simply follow the onscreen prompts.

continued

After you set up your AT&T wireless plan, you must then associate your iPhone with your Apple ID. You can obtain an Apple ID by purchasing items from the iTunes Store or by creating an account at the Apple Store Web site. If you are an AOL user, you can use your AOL username and password as your Apple ID.

If you do not yet have an Apple ID, you can leave the Apple ID and Password fields in the iTunes Account (Apple ID) screen blank and click Continue. iTunes prompts you to establish a username and password, and to indicate how you want to pay for any purchases you make at the iTunes Store.

⑬ Click to select whether or not you want to upgrade to more SMS text messages per month (◎ changes to ◉).

⑭ Click **Continue**.

The iTunes Account (Apple ID) screen appears.

⑮ Type your Apple ID.

⑯ Type your password.

⑰ Click **Continue**.

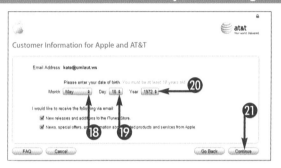

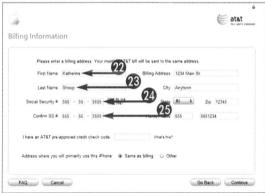

iTunes verifies your Apple ID and displays the Customer Information for Apple and AT&T screen.

**18** Click the **Month** ⟨⟩ and select your birth month.

**19** Click the **Day** ⟨⟩ and select your birth day.

**20** Click the **Year** ⟨⟩ and select your birth year.

**21** Click **Continue**.

The Billing Information screen appears.

**22** Type your first name.

**23** Type your last name.

**24** Type your Social Security Number.

**25** Type your Social Security Number a second time to confirm it.

### Attention!

Apple and AT&T require your Social Security Number in order to perform a credit check. However, many people are not comfortable providing their Social Security Number to Apple and AT&T — a legitimate concern, given the proliferation of identity theft. Other users — such as non-U.S. citizens — may not have Social Security Numbers. As an alternative, consider purchasing a pre-paid plan. For more information, contact Apple or AT&T.

continued

After you associate your iPhone with your Apple ID, you are prompted to provide your billing and other personal information. You are also required to agree to the terms in the license agreement. You should take a moment to read the license agreement carefully before you agree to its terms.

After you agree to the terms, you are ready to submit your information to Apple and AT&T in order to activate your iPhone and create your account. However, you should first take a moment to confirm that the information you typed is correct; to help you do this, iTunes displays a special screen that summarizes the information you have typed in.

26 Type your billing address.

27 Type your city.

28 Click the **State** and select the state in which you live.

29 Type your Zip Code.

30 Type your home phone number.

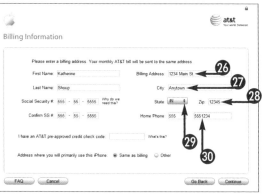

● If you have an AT&T pre-approved credit check code, you can type it here.

31 Click to indicate whether you intend to use your iPhone primarily at the billing address you typed ( changes to ).

32 Click **Continue**.

AT&T verifies that the address you typed is legitimate, and iTunes displays a license agreement.

㉝ Click **I have read and agree to the iPhone Terms and Conditions** (☐ changes to ☑).

㉞ Click **Continue**.

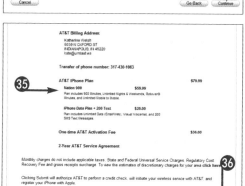

The Review Your Information screen appears.

㉟ Confirm that your information is correct.

㊱ Click **Submit**.

**Attention!**

If any information that appears in the Review Your Information screen is not correct, click the **Go Back** button as many times as needed to access the screen containing the field you need to change. If you have questions about the setup process, click the **FAQ** button to see a list of answers to frequently asked questions.

continued

After creating your account, you can sync your contacts, calendar entries, and e-mail messages to your iPhone. You can also sync media content, such as music, movies, audio books, and podcasts. The setup process automatically launches a sync operation when you reach the end.

Before launching the sync operation, you must specify what programs you use to manage contacts, calendars, e-mail, and bookmarks. Mac users must use Address Book or Yahoo! Address Book to port their contacts to their iPhone; iCal for calendars; Mail for e-mail; and Safari for bookmarks. PC users must use Yahoo! Address Book, Windows Address Book, Outlook Express, or Outlook to port their contacts; Outlook for calendar items; Outlook or Outlook Express for e-mail; and Safari or Internet Explorer for bookmarks.

The Completing Activation screen appears, informing you that when activation is complete, your iPhone will notify you.

㊲ Click **Continue** to set up and sync your iPhone.

The Set Up Your iPhone screen appears.

㊳ Type a name for your iPhone.

㊴ Click here to sync contacts, calendars, e-mail accounts, and bookmarks automatically (☐ changes to ☑).

㊵ Click the **Sync contacts from** ⬦ and then click the program that you use to store your contacts.

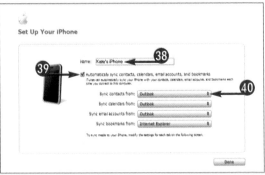

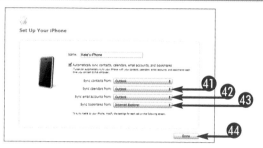

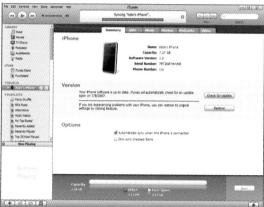

**41** Click the **Sync calendars from** ⟐ and then click the program that you use for your calendar.

**42** Click the **Sync email accounts from** ⟐ and then click your e-mail program.

**43** Click the **Sync bookmarks from** ⟐ and then click your Internet browser.

**44** Click **Done**.

iTunes syncs your iPhone, transferring your contact, calendar, e-mail, and bookmark data.

**Important!**

To inform you that activation is complete, and that your iPhone is ready to receive calls, AT&T sends a welcome text message to your iPhone. The activation process typically takes about 20 minutes, although it can take as long as several hours.

Suppose you want to download a movie file to your iPhone, but you are not certain that it has adequate space on its hard drive. Fortunately, Apple makes it easy to determine how much space is available on your iPhone. You can do so from within the Settings options of your iPhone.

The current generation of iPhones can store as much as 7.3GB of content. This is because, although they are advertised as having an 8GB hard drive, 700MB of that space is consumed by the iPhone operating system. Therefore, you can run out of space more quickly than you might have originally thought.

① Tap **Settings** (⚙).

The Settings screen appears.

② Tap **General**.

The General screen appears.

③ Tap **About**.

The About screen appears.

● The total capacity appears here.

● The amount of available space appears here.

④ Press the **Home** button to return to the main iPhone screen.

### More Options!

Another way to determine how much space is available on your iPhone is by connecting the iPhone to your computer. Click the **iPhone** entry in the iTunes Source list; iTunes displays a graphical representation of the available space on your iPhone in the bottom portion of the Summary tab.

When you connect your iPhone to your computer, the iPhone automatically syncs with iTunes by default. New music, movies, TV shows, podcasts, and photos are copied from your computer to your iPhone. Contacts and calendar entries sync both ways to ensure that both your computer and iPhone remain current.

If your computer stores more iTunes content than your iPhone can hold, you can specify exactly what items should be synced. You can also launch the sync operation manually by overriding the automatic sync setting.

You should not disconnect your iPhone from your computer during the sync process. You must wait for the operation to finish, click the Eject button next to the iPhone entry in the iTunes Source list, and then extract the cable from your iPhone.

---

① Connect your iPhone to your computer using the cable provided.

iTunes displays a special iPhone screen.

② To sync your iPhone manually rather than automatically, deselect **Automatically sync when this iPhone is connected** ( changes to ).

③ Click **Only sync checked items** to limit which items are transferred to the iPhone ( changes to ).

④ Click **Sync**.

● iTunes syncs your iPhone with the settings you established.

Apple may occasionally update the iPhone software to repair bugs or support new features. You can use iTunes to ensure that you have the most recent version of the iPhone software.

First, make sure that you are using the most up-to-date version of iTunes. To do so, connect to the Internet, click the iTunes Help menu, choose Check for Updates, and follow the onscreen

prompts. You are then ready to determine whether you have the most recent version of the Apple iPhone software.

You can also restore your iPhone to its factory settings, erasing all data on the iPhone. To do so, click the iPhone entry in the iTunes Source list, click the Summary tab in the screen that appears, and click the Restore button.

① Connect your iPhone to your computer using the cable provided.

iTunes displays a special iPhone screen.

② Click **Check for Update**.

iTunes indicates whether you are using the most recent version of iPhone software.

③ Click **OK**.

In this case, the iPhone software is up to date.

If your software is not up to date, you can click **Update** to install the latest version.

Although your iPhone is designed to be intuitive and easy to use, you may still encounter situations where you need help. You can access iPhone help from within iTunes if you are connected to the Internet. When you do, you are directed to a screen that enables you to access the Apple Web site, where you can find links to articles and tutorials.

Unfortunately, there is no help function on the iPhone, and so if you encounter a problem while traveling, you may not be able to troubleshoot using the iPhone as your help resource. However, if your Web browser is functioning and you can access the Internet, you can always browse the Apple Web site for help.

① In the iTunes window, click **Help**.

② Click **iPhone Help**.

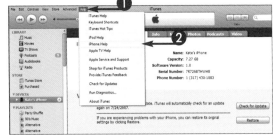

An iPhone Help window opens.

③ Click one of the links in the iPhone Help window.

This example selects **Service and Support**.

iTunes launches your Web browser and directs it to the page associated with the link you clicked in step 3.

④ Click a link to view the associated help information.

The help information appears.

**More Options!**

You can search for help information. To do so, open the iPhone Help window, click the **Show** button in the top-left corner, type a term for which you want to search, and click **List Topics**. The window lists instances of the keyword you typed; click an instance and then click **Display**. Information about the topic displays in the right pane, or links to pertinent information appear.

# Personalizing Your iPhone

You can personalize your iPhone in many ways. For example, you can apply a wallpaper to your iPhone, which is a background picture that displays when your iPhone is in sleep mode. You can choose from among several photos supplied by Apple or use one of your own.

You can also select a default ringtone. Apple provides several to choose from, ranging from a strumming guitar to a beeping robot.

To prevent others from using your iPhone without your permission, you can set a passcode lock. Similar to a PIN, you must enter the passcode to unlock the iPhone. Note that the iPhone includes an Emergency Call button for which the passcode is not required, enabling others to dial your iPhone in the event of an emergency.

You can adjust settings such as the brightness of your iPhone screen and whether the iPhone emits a sound to notify you of various events, such as the receipt of a voicemail or SMS message.

# Quick Tips

# Change Auto-Lock Settings

By default, the Auto-Lock feature places the iPhone in sleep mode. When your iPhone is in sleep mode, the screen deactivates and becomes unresponsive. To unlock, or wake, the iPhone, you must press the Home button below the iPhone screen, tap the arrow that appears on the screen, and drag it from left to right.

You can easily change the amount of time that your iPhone waits to engage the Auto-Lock feature. For example, you can change the setting from the default 1 Minute setting to 2 Minutes, 3 Minutes, 4 Minutes, 5 Minutes, or Never. *Note: The longer the iPhone is awake, the more battery power it consumes.*

① In the main iPhone screen, tap **Settings** (⚙).

The Settings screen appears.

② Tap **General**.

The General screen appears.

③ Tap **Auto-Lock**.

The Auto-Lock screen appears.

④ Tap the desired Auto-Lock setting.

⑤ Press the **Home** button to change the setting and return to the main iPhone screen.

### Did You Know?

When you engage the Auto-Lock feature, you do not need a special passcode to unlock your iPhone. However, if you want to lock your iPhone, thereby preventing others from using it, you can use the Passcode Lock feature. For more information on the Passcode Lock feature, see the "Set a Passcode Lock" section.

To prevent others from using your iPhone, enable the Passcode Lock feature. When you do, you establish a four-digit combination, which you then use to unlock the iPhone whenever it is turned on or wakes from sleep. Alternatively, you can unlock your iPhone by connecting it to your primary computer; when you disconnect, the iPhone screen is no longer locked.

If you forget your passcode and you do not have access to your primary computer, your only option is to restore the iPhone to its factory settings, which erases the device's contents. To do so, connect the iPhone to any computer on which iTunes is installed, click the iPhone in the Source list in iTunes, and then click the Restore button in the iPhone Summary screen.

① In the iPhone Settings screen, tap **General**.

***Note:*** *To access the iPhone Settings screen, tap **Settings** (⚙) in the main iPhone screen.*

The General screen appears.

② Tap **Passcode Lock**.

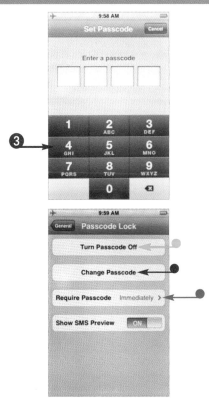

If no passcode has been established, your iPhone prompts you to select the desired passcode.

③ Type the passcode you want to use.

④ When prompted, type the passcode a second time to confirm it.

The Passcode Lock screen appears.

● You can tap **Turn Passcode Off** to disable the passcode.

● You can tap **Change Passcode** to change the passcode.

● You can specify whether a passcode should be required immediately or after a specific time.

⑤ Press the **Home** button to confirm the changes and return to the main iPhone screen.

### Did You Know?

There may be times when you want others to be able to dial out using your iPhone — for example, if you are unconscious and in need of medical attention. For this reason, the iPhone includes a special Emergency Call button in the Enter Passcode screen, which is the screen you use to enter your four-digit passcode. Tapping this **Emergency Call** button reveals the iPhone keypad.

# Choose a Ringtone

You can choose from among several ringtones as the default for incoming calls. You can also assign specific ringtones to individual contacts.

There may be times when you do not want your iPhone to emit a ringtone — for example, if you are at a movie. To disable the ringtone, you can toggle the Ring/Silent switch on the side of the

iPhone. For help locating this switch, refer to Chapter 1. When the switch is aligned with the volume buttons on the side of the iPhone, it is set to ring; when the switch is offset from the volume buttons, it is in silent mode. You can also set up your iPhone to vibrate; for more information, see the next task.

① In the main iPhone screen, tap **Settings** (⚙).

The Settings screen appears.

② Tap **Sounds**.

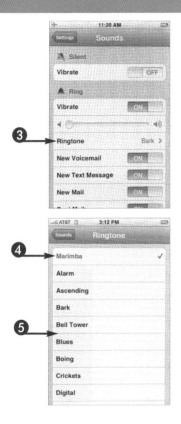

The Sounds screen appears.

③ Tap **Ringtone**.

The Ringtone screen appears.

④ Tap a ringtone to listen to it.

● A check mark (✓) appears next to the ringtone you touched, indicating that it is selected.

⑤ Repeat step **4** to listen to other ringtones.

⑥ When you find a ringtone you like, press the **Home** button.

iPhone sets the selected ringtone as the default and returns you to the main iPhone screen.

### Did You Know?

As great as Apple's ringtones are, you may well prefer to personalize your ringtone — for example, by using your favorite song. To this end, Apple enables you to convert songs you purchase from the iTunes Store into ringtones. For more information, see the task "Convert a Song to a Ringtone" in Chapter 6.

The iPhone emits sounds when you receive a new voicemail, text, or e-mail message; when you send an e-mail message; when a calendar alert is issued; when your iPhone locks; and when you tap a key on the onscreen keyboard. If you would prefer not to hear these sounds, you can silence the iPhone.

You can also specify whether the iPhone should vibrate when it is in silent mode and/or in ring mode, and the maximum volume for your ringtone. You switch between ring and silent mode by toggling the Ring/Silent switch on the side of the iPhone. While in silent mode, the iPhone does not play back rings, alerts, or other sounds, although it does play back alarms that you set using the clock.

① In the iPhone Settings screen, tap **Sounds**.

***Note:*** *To access the iPhone Settings screen, tap ▣ in the main iPhone screen.*

The Sounds screen appears.

② Tap the **ON/OFF** option of any feature to toggle the sound on or off.

● You can tap here to toggle the Vibrate setting in silent mode.

● You can tap here to toggle the Vibrate setting in ring mode.

● You can drag the slider to adjust the volume of the ringtone.

③ Press the **Home** button to confirm the changes and return to the main iPhone screen.

Your iPhone can store hours of video content, and you can enjoy this content on the high-quality screen. Although the screen is small, it is surprisingly vibrant, resulting in a pleasurable, if not immersive, viewing experience.

You can adjust various screen settings, such as brightness, to improve video

playback. However, if you increase the screen's brightness, the amount of time your iPhone can operate between charges is reduced.

To conserve battery life, you can use the Auto-Brightness setting, which adjusts the screen's brightness to accommodate existing lighting conditions.

① In the iPhone Settings screen, tap **Brightness**.

*Note: To access the iPhone Settings screen, tap* 🔲 *in the main iPhone screen.*

The Brightness screen appears.

② Drag the slider to brighten or darken the screen.

③ Tap here to toggle the Auto Brightness feature off and on.

④ Press the **Home** button to confirm the changes and return to the main iPhone screen.

A great way to personalize your iPhone is to apply wallpaper. Wallpaper is a background picture that displays when you lock your iPhone. Wallpaper also appears in the background when you place a phone call to a contact with whom you have not associated a photo.

When applying wallpaper to your iPhone, you can choose from among several

photos supplied by Apple. You can also use one of your own photos. This might be a photo that you uploaded from your computer to your iPhone, or one that you created using the built-in camera function. To learn more about uploading photos to your iPhone, as well as using your iPhone as a camera, see Chapter 8.

① In the iPhone Settings screen, tap **Wallpaper**.

*Note:* To access the iPhone Settings screen, tap 📷 in the main iPhone screen.

The Wallpaper screen appears.

② Tap the folder containing the image you want to use as your wallpaper.

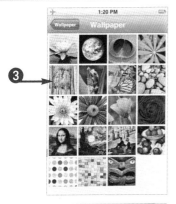

A screen appears with thumbnail versions of the images in the selected folder.

③ Tap the image you want to apply as wallpaper.

The Wallpaper Preview screen appears.

● A preview of the wallpaper displays.

④ Tap **Set Wallpaper** to apply the image you selected.

⑤ Press the **Home** button to confirm the changes and return to the main iPhone screen.

**Did You Know?**

You can select from professional-grade images provided by Apple. These appear in the Wallpaper folder, accessible via the Wallpaper screen. Available images range from a photo of Planet Earth to a reproduction of Vincent Van Gogh's "Starry Starry Night."

# Using Your iPhone as a PDA

Your iPhone can be used for many different purposes, including as a cell phone, a music player, a video player, and web browser. In addition, it can act as a personal digital assistant, or PDA. You can use it to store information about your contacts as well as to maintain a calendar.

Depending on what type of contacts-management and calendar programs you use on your computer, you may be able to sync, or copy, the contacts and calendar entries that you maintain on your computer

to your iPhone. The iPhone can work with the following contacts programs: Mac OS X Address Book (Mac), Yahoo! Address Book (Mac or PC), Windows Address Book (PC), Outlook Express (PC), or Outlook (PC). It also supports the iCal (Mac) and Outlook (PC) calendar programs.

In addition to syncing contacts and calendars to your iPhone from these programs, you can add entries to both the iPhone Contacts and Calendar features from directly within your iPhone.

# Quick Tips

Assuming you use one of the following contacts programs on your computer, you can copy the contacts stored on your computer to your iPhone: Mac OS X Address Book (Mac), Yahoo! Address Book (Mac or PC), Windows Address Book (PC), Outlook Express (PC), or Outlook (PC).

You transfer your contacts to your iPhone through a sync operation. Any new contacts you add to your contacts program are ported to your iPhone the next time you sync. If your contacts program allows you to associate a photo with a contact, that photo will also appear with the contact on your iPhone.

You can also add contacts directly to your iPhone. Entries added in this way are merged into your computer's address book during the next sync operation.

## SYNCHRONIZE CONTACTS

**1** Connect your iPhone to your computer.

**2** In iTunes, click the entry for your iPhone.

**3** Click the **Info** tab.

**4** Click **Sync contacts from** (☐ changes to ☑).

**5** Click the **Sync contacts from** and select the program you use to manage contacts on your computer.

**6** Click **Apply**.

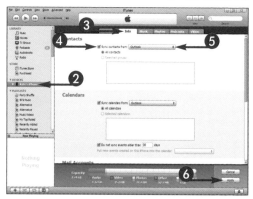

## VIEW CONTACTS

**1** In the main iPhone screen, tap **Phone** (📞).

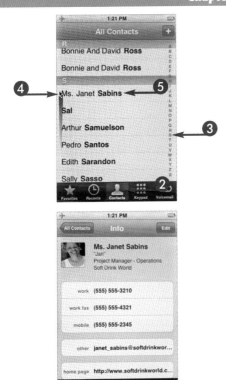

2 Tap **Contacts** ().

A list appears of contacts stored on your iPhone.

3 Tap the first letter of the contact's name.

4 Drag your finger up or down to locate the contact.

5 When you locate the contact you want to view, tap it.

iPhone displays information about the contact.

**TIP**

**Did You Know?**
If you use a Mac, and you have set up the OS X Address Book to sync with another address book, such as Microsoft Entourage, then that address book also syncs with your iPhone.

If you enter a new contact into your computer's contacts program, then that contact will be added to your iPhone the next time you sync. You can also add a contact directly into your iPhone. The next time you sync, that contact will be merged into your computer's contacts program.

When adding a contact to your iPhone, you can supply any of the following information: the contact's name, a photo, phone numbers, e-mail addresses, Web site addresses, and street addresses. Of course, you are not required to enter *all* of this information for a contact. To create a contact entry, only a name is required. However, adding more information will help you to keep track of your contacts.

---

① In the main iPhone screen, tap **Phone** (📞).

② Tap **Contacts** (👤).

A list of contacts stored on your iPhone displays.

③ Tap ➕.

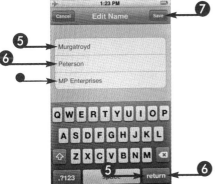

The New Contact screen appears.

● You can tap here to add a phone number to the contact entry.

● You can tap here to add an e-mail address to the contact entry.

● You can tap here to add a URL to the contact entry.

● You can tap here to add an address to the contact entry.

❹ Tap the **First Last** field.

❺ Type the contact's first name and then tap **Return**.

❻ Type the contact's last name and then tap **Return**.

● You can also type the name of the company where the contact works.

❼ Tap **Save**.

❽ In the New Contact screen, tap **Save** again.

The contact is added.

**Did You Know?**

You can add more fields to a contact entry. These include Prefix, Middle (name), Suffix, Nickname, Job Title, Department, and Birthday. To do so, tap **Add Field** in the New Contact screen, choose the field you want to add, and enter the desired information in the field.

The iPhone displays the appropriate screen to enable you to populate the field. This example displays the Edit Phone screen.

③ Type the contact's information.

***Note:*** *When adding a phone number, to indicate whether it is the contact's home number, work number, or a different number altogether, tap* ⟩ *above the keypad and select the appropriate entry in the screen that appears.*

④ Tap **Save**.

● The record is updated to reflect your changes.

⑤ Tap **Done**.

### Remove It!

To remove information from a contact record, tap ⊖ next to the field that contains the data you want to remove, and tap the **Delete** button that appears. To delete an entire contact entry, drag your finger to scroll to the bottom of the record and then tap the **Delete Contact** button that appears.

For many people, putting a face to a name can be difficult. To help, iPhone enables you to associate a photograph with a contact record. Then, whenever you receive a phone call from that person or view his or her contact record, the photo you selected displays.

If you like, you can use a photo that you have uploaded from your computer to your iPhone. You can also take a photo using the built-in camera function. To learn more about the photo and camera tools, see Chapter 8.

You can associate a photo with a contact from within the screen used to edit a contact record. To access this screen, first open the contact. Then tap the Edit button in the screen that appears.

① In the contact's Info screen, tap **Add Photo**.

② Tap **Choose Existing Photo**.

*Note: To take a photo of your contact, tap **Take Photo** instead of Choose Existing Photo, compose your photograph, and then tap the green button that appears. The iPhone captures the image. If you like it, tap **Set Photo**; otherwise, tap **Retake** and repeat.*

The Photo Albums screen appears.

③ Tap the album that contains the image you want to use.

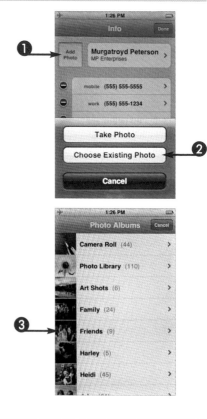

A screen appears, displaying thumbnail versions of the images in the selected album.

④ Tap the image you want to associate with the contact.

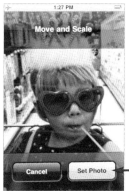

You can use your fingers to resize the photo.

⑤ Tap **Set Photo**.

Your iPhone associates the selected photo with the contact record.

**More Options!**

Another way to associate an image with a contact is to do the following:

① Tap **Photos** (📷) on the main iPhone screen.

② Tap the photo album that contains the photo you want to use.

③ Tap the photo you want to use.

④ Tap 🖼 in the bottom-left corner of the screen.

⑤ Tap **Assign to Contact**.

⑥ Locate and tap the contact in the screen that appears.

⑦ Tap **Set Photo**.

The photo is associated with the contact.

In addition to choosing a default ringtone for your iPhone (for more information, refer to the task "Choose a Ringtone" in Chapter 2), you can assign specific ringtones to various contacts. Then, when the contact calls, you will hear the ringtone you selected, which acts as an audio cue to tell you who is calling.

Apple offers several built-in ringtones; in addition, you can convert songs purchased from the iTunes Store into ringtones. (For more information, see the task "Convert a Song to a Ringtone" in Chapter 6.)

You can associate a ringtone with a contact from within the contact record. To open a contact, see the section, "Synchronize and View Contacts."

① In the contact's Info screen, tap **Edit**.

② Tap **Assign Ringtone**.

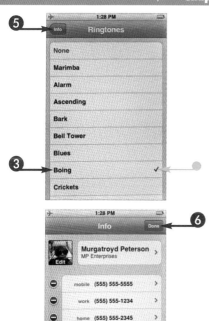

The Ringtones screen appears.

③ Tap a ringtone to listen to it.

● A check mark appears next to the ringtone you touched, indicating that it is selected.

④ Repeat step **3** to listen to additional ringtones.

⑤ When you have selected the ringtone you want to use, tap **Info**.

● The tone you selected displays here.

⑥ Tap **Done**.

*Note: A faster way to save your selected ringtone is to tap the Home button after choosing the tone you want to use. The iPhone saves the change and returns you to its main screen.*

**Important!**

To disable the ringer, toggle the Ring/Silent switch on the side of the phone. When the switch is aligned with the volume buttons on the side of the iPhone, it is set to ring; when the switch is offset from the volume buttons, it is in silent mode. For example, you might put your iPhone in silent mode if you are at a movie or in an important meeting.

By the time you sync the contacts you maintain on your computer with your iPhone and then add more contacts to the iPhone itself, you may well have hundreds of contacts stored on the device.

If your iPhone contains a large number of contact entries, you may find it annoying to sort through all of those entries each time you want to use your iPhone. To avoid this, you can designate certain contacts, such as your spouse, your best friend, your boss, and so on, as favorites. These contacts are listed in their own separate, smaller list, making it easier to locate the contacts you access most often. *Note: Tapping a contact in the Favorites list does not open the contact's record; rather, it initiates a phone call to the contact.*

① In the All Contacts screen, tap the contact you want to designate as a Favorite.

**Note:** *To open the All Contacts screen, tap **Phone** ( ) in the main iPhone screen, and if necessary, tap **Contacts** ( ).*

An Info screen appears, containing information about the contact.

② Tap **Add to Favorites**.

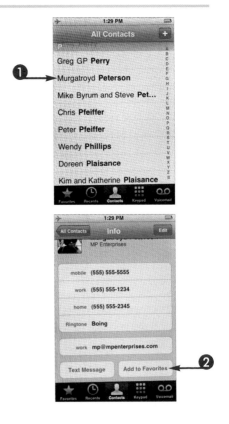

If the contact record contains multiple phone numbers, iPhone prompts you to specify which number should be added to the Favorites list.

③ Tap the number you want to add.

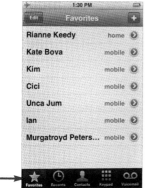

④ To see the Favorites list, tap **Favorites** ().

iPhone displays contacts that have been designated as Favorites.

---

**TIP**

**Remove It!**

To remove a contact from your Favorites list, tap the **Edit** button in the Favorites screen, tap ⊖ next to the contact entry, tap the **Remove** button that appears, and then tap **Done**. The contact is removed from the Favorites list, but remains in the main Contacts list.

If you use iCal (Mac) or Outlook (PC) to maintain your calendar on your computer, you can port your calendar entries to your iPhone.

You transfer your calendar entries to your iPhone through a sync operation. Any new calendar entries that you add to your computer's calendar program are ported to your iPhone the next time you sync.

In addition to adding entries to your calendar using your computer, you can add them using your iPhone; entries that you add in this way are merged into the calendar on your computer during the next sync operation.

Your iPhone can emit a sound notification as calendar events draw near. For information on how you can disable the sound notification, see Chapter 2.

### SYNC CALENDAR ITEMS

1. Connect your iPhone to your computer.

2. Click the entry for your iPhone.

3. Click the **Info** tab.

4. Click **Sync calendars from** (☐ changes to ☑).

5. Click the **Sync calendars from** ⬧ and select the program you use to manage calendars on your computer.

6. Click **Apply**.

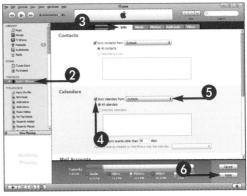

### VIEW CALENDARS

1. In the main iPhone screen, tap **Calendar** (📅).

The calendar opens.

● The calendar entries appear in List view.

② To switch to a different view, tap **Day** or **Month**.

The calendar view changes.

*Note: To view details about a calendar event, simply tap it in the Calendar screen; iPhone displays information about the event in a new screen.*

**Attention!**

To delete an event, tap it in the calendar to open it in a separate screen, tap the **Edit** button in the upper-right corner, tap **Delete Event**, and tap **Delete Event** again to confirm the deletion. If the event is recurring, iPhone prompts you to specify whether this instance of the event should be deleted or whether all future events should be removed. Choose the desired option.

The Calendar function enables you to plan your days by entering calendar events. An event can be a one-time appointment, such as a luncheon, or a recurring event, such as a weekly meeting.

When you create a new appointment, you can enter a title for the appointment, a start time, an end time, and, optionally,

a repeat interval. Interval options include Every Day, Every Week, Every 2 Weeks, Every Month, and Every Year.

In addition, you can specify whether your iPhone should emit a sound notification to alert you when your appointment draws near, and specify when that alert should sound.

① In the calendar screen, tap ![+] in the upper-right corner.

*Note: To access the calendar screen, tap Calendar (![22]) in the main iPhone screen.*

The Add Event screen appears.

② Tap the **Title Location** field.

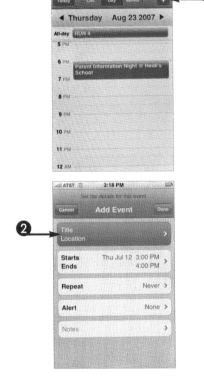

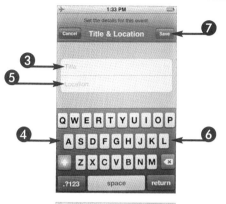

The Title & Location screen appears.

**③** Tap the **Title** field.

**④** Type a title for the calendar event.

**⑤** Tap the **Location** field.

**⑥** Type a location for the event.

**⑦** Tap **Save**.

**⑧** In the Add Event screen, tap the **Starts Ends** field.

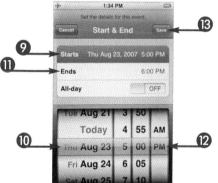

The Start & End screen appears.

**⑨** Tap the **Starts** field.

**⑩** Flick the screen to spin the date, hour, minute, and AM/PM portions of the wheel to the desired start time.

**⑪** Tap the **Ends** field.

**⑫** Flick the screen to spin the date, hour, minute, and AM/PM portions of the wheel to the desired end time.

**⑬** Tap **Save**.

**⑭** In the Add Event screen, tap **Done**.

iPhone adds the event.

**More Options!**

To set an alert for the event, tap the **Alert** field in the Add Event screen and specify when the alert should sound: 5, 15, or 30 minutes before; 1 or 2 hours before; 1 or 2 days before; or on the date of the event. When you are finished, tap **Save**. If you add an alert, iPhone gives you the opportunity to add a second alert; follow the same steps.

If you want to add to or otherwise change the information in a calendar event, you can easily do so. One way is to make the necessary changes using your computer's calendar program and then sync your iPhone with your computer. An easier way is to make changes to an appointment from within your iPhone.

Editing an existing event is similar to adding a new one: You can enter a title and location for the event; set a start or end time; specify whether the event is recurring and, if so, at what interval; set an alert; and enter notes about the upcoming event.

① In the calendar screen, tap the event you want to edit.

*Note:* To access the calendar screen, tap *Calendar (📅) in the main iPhone screen.*

An Event screen appears, with details about the event listed.

② Tap **Edit**.

The Edit screen appears.

③ Tap a field in the Edit screen to enter the necessary information.

④ Tap **Done**.

● The changes you entered are reflected in the Event screen.

In this example, an alert is set.

⑤ Press the **Home** button to confirm your changes and return to the main iPhone screen.

**Try This!**

To add a note to an event, tap the **Notes** field in the Edit screen. In the Notes screen that appears, use the keyboard to type any notes, and then tap **Save** to return to the Edit screen.

# Using Your iPhone as a Mobile Phone

When the cell-signal indicator at the top of the iPhone screen shows that you have access to the cell network, you can use your iPhone to make and receive phone calls.

You can access mobile-phone features by tapping the Phone button on the main iPhone screen. When you do this, your iPhone displays a series of buttons along the bottom of the screen: Favorites, Recents, Contacts, Keypad, and Voicemail. Tapping these buttons enables you to access contacts that you have designated as

Favorites, entries for calls you have recently made or received, a list of all contacts stored in your iPhone, a numeric keypad for dialing manually, and a list of voicemail messages that you have received.

In addition to making and receiving calls, you can change the phone-related settings as needed. For example, you can set up call-forwarding, disable call-waiting, and hide your caller ID information if you want to keep it private. You access various phone settings from the iPhone Settings screen.

# Quick Tips

# Place a Call

You can place a call on your iPhone by locating the record for the person you want to call in Contacts. Another way to place a call is to dial the number using the keypad. To display the keypad, tap the Phone button on the main iPhone screen and tap the Keypad button in the screen that appears.

If you have recently used your iPhone to speak with the person you want to reach, that person may appear in the Recents screen. If so, you can launch your call from there by simply tapping the contact's entry. Likewise, if the person appears in either the Voicemail or Favorites screen, you can launch the call from there.

**①** In the main iPhone screen, tap **Phone** ().

**②** Tap **Contacts** (   ).

**③** Flick the screen to scroll up or down to locate your contact name.

**④** Tap the name of the contact you want to call.

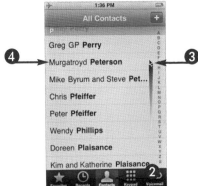

iPhone displays information about the contact.

⑤ Tap the number you want to call.

iPhone places the call.

⑥ To hang up, tap **End Call**.

**More Options!**

When you place a call, your iPhone displays a series of onscreen buttons that you can tap to perform different tasks. You can mute the iPhone microphone, display the keypad, switch to speaker mode, phone a third party, place the person with whom you are speaking on hold, or display your contacts to locate a third party's phone number.

When you receive an incoming call, your iPhone rings, vibrates, or does both. If the caller is a contact with whom you have associated a photo, the photo also displays.

You can answer the call immediately, or press the Sleep/Wake button to silence the ringer before answering. Alternatively, you can decline the call by tapping the Decline button or by pressing the

Sleep/Wake button twice quickly, which directs the caller to your voicemail.

If you are already on the phone, iPhone displays buttons that you can tap to respond to the call. For example, you can ignore it, which directs the caller to your voicemail; place the existing caller on hold and answer the incoming call; or end the current call and answer the incoming one.

① When you receive an incoming call, tap **Answer**.

*Note: If your phone is locked when you receive a call, drag the slider that appears on the screen to answer the call.*

iPhone connects the call.

② To end the call, tap **End Call**.

You can use your iPhone hands-free in a number of situations, such as while driving or while on hold. One way to speak hands-free on your iPhone is to use the special stereo headset that came with the device, which features a built-in microphone. If you use your stereo headphones to listen to music or other content on your iPhone, and you receive a call, you hear the ringtone through the headset. You can answer the call by squeezing the microphone portion of the headset until it clicks.

Another way to speak hands-free is to switch the iPhone to speaker mode.

① While on a call, tap **Speaker** (🔊).

The iPhone switches to speaker mode.

② To switch speaker mode off, tap **Speaker** again.

If you are already on a call, you can connect with an additional person by tapping the recipient's entry in the Favorites list, the Recents list, or the Contacts list, or by using the number keypad. For example, you might place additional calls to plan a get-together with a few friends, or to engage in a conference call for work.

When you place a call while already on the phone, the person on the initial call is placed on hold, enabling you to speak with the person on the additional line privately. You can then choose to merge the calls together, enabling all parties to hear the conversation.

① While on a call, tap **Add Call** (➕).

The Create a New Call screen appears.

② Tap **Keypad**.

③ Type the telephone number of the person you want to call.

④ Tap **Call**.

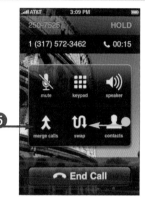

The iPhone launches the new call, placing the first call on hold.

● To switch to the first call, you can tap **Swap**.

⑤ To merge the calls, tap **Merge Calls**.

Your iPhone merges the calls into a conference call.

**Did You Know?**

You are not limited to three-way calling; you can merge as many as five calls. To add more calls to an existing conference call, simply repeat the steps in this task.

If you decline an incoming call or are unavailable to answer it, callers are directed to your voicemail. This feature plays a greeting and then enables the caller to leave a message.

You access these messages from the Voicemail screen, where you can view entries for voicemail messages and listen to them in any order. You are not required to listen to a series of options

or to other messages in order to access the one you want. You can also access a caller's contact record from an entry in the Voicemail screen.

After you listen to a voicemail message, your iPhone saves it for 30 days, by default. To delete a message, you can tap its entry in the list and then tap the Delete button that appears.

---

① Tap **Phone** ( ) on the main iPhone screen.

● If you have missed any calls or received any voicemails, the Phone button on the main iPhone screen indicates the number of calls and voicemails.

● The Voicemail button indicates how many unheard voicemails you have received.

② Tap **Voicemail** ( ).

The Voicemail screen appears.

● New voicemails are marked with a blue circle.

③ Tap an entry in the Voicemail screen.

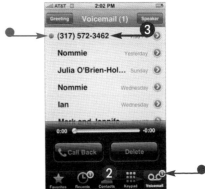

Your iPhone plays back the voicemail message.

- To hear the message in speaker mode, you can tap **Speaker**.

- You can drag to move forward or backward through a message to review it.

- To delete the message, you can tap **Delete**.

- To view the caller's contact record, tap 📎.

④ To call back the person who left the message, you can tap **Call Back**.

The iPhone dials the number associated with the voicemail message.

**Did You Know?**

You can check your iPhone voicemails from another phone. To do so, use the phone to call your number. When your voicemail greeting begins to play, tap the * key, type your voicemail password (you established this when you set up your voicemail), tap the # key, and then follow the instructions.

If you receive a call from someone who has not been entered as a contact, only the phone number appears in the call's entry in the Recents and Voicemail screens. You can create a new contact record from the entry in either screen; that way, subsequent calls from the number will be flagged with the contact's name.

If someone for whom you have already created a contact entry phones you, but from a phone number that you have not yet entered into the record, you can add the new number to the existing record. Again, you can do this from either the Recents screen or the Voicemail screen.

---

① In the Recents or Voicemail screen, tap ⊙ for the entry you want to use as the basis for a new contact.

An Unknown screen appears.

② Tap **Create New Contact**.

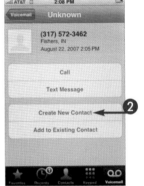

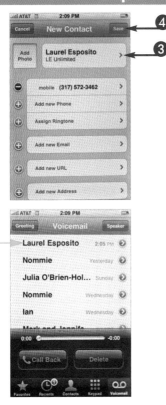

The New Contact screen appears.

③ Add contact information as needed.

*Note:* For more information about creating new contacts, see Chapter 3.

④ Tap **Save**.

Your iPhone creates a new contact record.

● The entry in the Voicemail or Recents list is updated to reflect the contact information.

**More Options!**

If someone for whom you have already created a contact entry phones you from a new or different phone number, you can add this number to the existing contact record. To do so, tap **Add to Existing Contact**. Then locate and tap the contact record to which you want to add the number, specify whether the number is a mobile number, home number, or other type, and tap **Save**.

If you will be away from your iPhone for a period of time, you can set it up to forward calls that it receives to a different number. For example, you might forward calls when you are on vacation, and you do not want to bring your iPhone with you.

The iPhone saves the last number you entered in the Call Forwarding screen,

which means that you can reuse it. This is useful if, for example, you frequently forward calls to a particular number; if it was the last number you entered in the Call Forwarding screen, you can simply select it rather than entering the number again.

① In the iPhone Settings screen, tap **Phone**.

**Note:** To access the iPhone Settings screen, tap **Settings** ( ) in the main iPhone screen.

The Phone screen appears.

② Tap **Call Forwarding**.

The Call Forwarding screen appears.

③ Tap **Off**.

The Call Forwarding option toggles from Off to On.

● The last number to which calls were forwarded from your iPhone appears here.

④ To change the number to which calls will be forwarded, tap **Forwarding To**.

The Forwarding To screen appears.

⑤ Type the number to which you want calls to be forwarded.

⑥ Tap **Call Forwarding**.

⑦ Press the **Home** button to change the setting and return to the main iPhone screen.

### Important!

Calls to your iPhone are forwarded only if your iPhone is in the range of your cell-phone network at the time you set it up to forward calls. If you are outside the provider's range of coverage, then calls are not forwarded.

By default, call waiting is enabled on the iPhone. However, if you do not want your calls interrupted, you can disable this setting, either permanently or temporarily. For example, you might disable the setting temporarily if you will be on an important call during which you do not want to be interrupted.

If you disable call waiting, any calls you receive while you are already on the phone are directed to voicemail. For information on listening to voicemails, see the section, "Listen to a Voicemail Message." To re-enable call waiting, simply repeat the steps in this task to toggle the option back on.

① In the main iPhone screen, tap **Settings** (⚙️).

The Settings screen appears.

② Tap **Phone**.

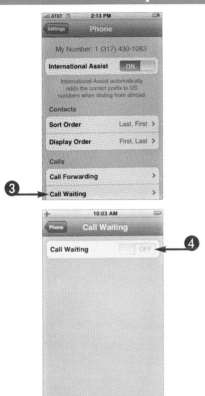

The Phone screen appears.

③ Tap **Call Waiting**.

The Call Waiting screen appears.

④ Tap **On**.

The Call Waiting option toggles from On to Off.

⑤ Press the **Home** button to change the setting and return to the main iPhone screen.

**More Options!**

To keep your number private when you phone others, you can hide your caller ID information. To do so, tap **Show My Caller ID** in the Phone screen. Then, in the Show My Caller ID screen, tap **On** to toggle the Show My Caller ID option off. When you are finished, tap the **Home** button to change the setting and return to the main iPhone screen.

# Sending and Receiving E-Mail and Text Messages with Your iPhone

Over the last several years, e-mail and text messaging have become primary methods of communicating. If you have access either to the AT&T Edge network or to a wireless network, you can use your iPhone to send and receive e-mail and text messages. To determine whether you have access to a network, look for a small E or a WiFi symbol along the top of the iPhone screen.

When you reply to an e-mail or text message, or create a new e-mail or text message, the iPhone displays an onscreen keyboard. This predictive and intelligent feature automatically suggests corrections as you type. To use a correction suggested by the iPhone, tap the Spacebar, a punctuation key, or the Return key on the onscreen keyboard. To reject the correction, simply keep typing. After you reject a suggested correction twice, iPhone adds the word to its dictionary and does not suggest the correction again.

# Add an E-Mail Account

If you use Mail, Entourage, Outlook, or Outlook Express for e-mail, your iPhone automatically detects any e-mail accounts that you have set up on your computer. It then copies the necessary information when you sync your iPhone with your computer.

To set up your iPhone to sync with your e-mail accounts, connect your iPhone to your computer. Click the entry for the iPhone in the iTunes Source list, click the Info tab, select the Sync Selected Mail Accounts From check box, choose your computer's e-mail program, click the check box next to the account you want to sync, and then click Apply.

You can also add e-mail accounts manually. When you do, the account settings are not copied to your computer when you sync.

---

① Tap **Mail** in the Settings screen.

*Note:* *To access the Settings screen, tap* **Settings** *(⚙) in the main iPhone screen.*

The Mail screen appears.

② Tap **Add Account**.

The Add Account screen appears.

③ Tap the name of your e-mail account provider.

This example selects **Gmail**.

*Note: If your e-mail account is with Gmail, you may need to perform additional steps on the Gmail Web site to enable it for use with your iPhone. For more information, see the Gmail help information.*

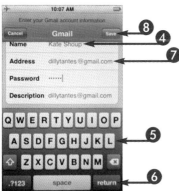

④ Tap the **Name** field.

A keyboard appears.

⑤ Type the name that you want to appear in the Sender field of outgoing messages.

⑥ Tap **Return**.

⑦ Repeat steps **4** to **6** to enter the e-mail address, password, and, optionally, a description of the account.

⑧ Tap **Save**.

The account is added to your iPhone.

### Important!

If your account is with a provider other than the ones listed in the Add Account screen, tap **Other** and enter the following information: the address of your Internet service provider's incoming and outgoing mail servers, your username and password, and whether it is a POP, IMAP, or Exchange account. If you do not have this information, contact your Internet service provider.

# Set the Default E-Mail Account

If your iPhone is set up to use multiple e-mail accounts, you can choose the account you want to use from within the Mail program whenever you send a message. Even so, you should specify which account should serve as the default; this default account is the one that you will use when you choose to send an e-mail message using the non-Mail applications on your iPhone — for example, when you decide to send a digital picture to someone from within the Photos application or to share a link to a video on YouTube with a friend. You can set the default e-mail account through the Settings screen on your iPhone.

① Tap **Settings** (📱) in the main iPhone screen.

The Settings screen appears.

② Tap **Mail**.

The Mail screen appears.

③ Tap **Default Account**.

The Default Account screen appears.

④ Tap the account you want to set as the default.

⑤ Press the **Home** button under the iPhone screen.

The iPhone saves your changes and returns you to the main screen.

### Remove It!

To delete an e-mail account from your iPhone, tap **Settings** (🔘) in the main iPhone screen, tap **Mail**, tap the account you want to remove, and tap **Delete Account**. When you delete an account from your iPhone, it does not affect the status of that account on the computer you use to sync your iPhone.

# Retrieve and View E-Mail Messages

When you open the Inbox for an e-mail account on your iPhone, your iPhone determines whether your e-mail account provider's mail server has received any new messages for you. If so, it downloads them.

If you like, you can set up your iPhone to check for new messages automatically at the time interval you specify. (Note that if you have a Yahoo! e-mail account,

messages you receive via that account will be transferred automatically to your iPhone as soon as they reach the Yahoo! server.)

Your iPhone can play a sound when you receive new messages. Additionally, the Mail button on the main iPhone screen indicates whether, and how many, unread messages have been downloaded to your iPhone.

---

**①** Tap **Mail** (📧).

● The Mail button (📧) on the main iPhone screen indicates how many new e-mail messages you have received.

**②** Tap **Inbox**.

*Note:* If you have set up your iPhone to manage multiple e-mail accounts, you may need to first tap the account whose Inbox you want to view.

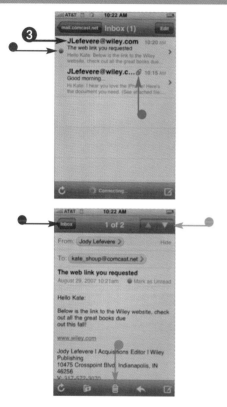

Your iPhone displays the messages in the account's Inbox.

● New messages are marked with a blue circle.

● Messages containing attachments are marked with a paperclip icon.

❸ Tap a message to view it.

Your iPhone displays the contents of the message.

● You can tap ▲ or ▼ to view the next or previous message in the Inbox.

● You can tap **Inbox** to return to the Inbox.

● To delete the message, you can tap **Delete** (🗑).

## Try This!

To configure your iPhone to automatically check for and retrieve new e-mail messages, tap **Settings** (⚙) on the main iPhone screen, tap **Mail**, tap **Auto-Check**, and then tap **Every 15 Minutes**, **Every 30 Minutes**, or **Every Hour**. To set up your iPhone to play a sound whenever you receive new e-mail, tap **Settings** (⚙) on the main iPhone screen, tap **Sound**, and toggle the New Mail option to **On**.

When someone wants to send you a file — for example, a document containing a travel itinerary or other important information — the sender can do so by attaching it to an e-mail message.

If you receive an e-mail that contains an attachment, you may be able to view the attachment on your iPhone. Some of the supported file types include the following:

Microsoft Word (.doc and .docx), Microsoft Excel (.xls and .xlsx), Adobe PDF (.pdf), text files (.txt), and HTML files (.htm and .html).

If you receive an attachment that you cannot view on your iPhone, you will be able to see the name of the file, but you will not be able to open it.

① With the message containing the attachment open in your iPhone, tap the entry for the attachment.

If the file type is supported by your iPhone, the attachment opens.

People often send e-mail messages that contain links to Web sites or other files on the Internet. If you receive a message containing a link through your iPhone, you can tap the link to access the Web page or site that it targets.

In most cases, when you tap a link, iPhone launches the Safari Web browser and directs you to the appropriate page,

although links can also perform other functions, such as directing you to a map or dialing a phone number. After you follow a link, you can return to the e-mail containing the link by tapping the Home button and then tapping the Mail button.

Text links in an e-mail message received through your iPhone are typically underlined in blue.

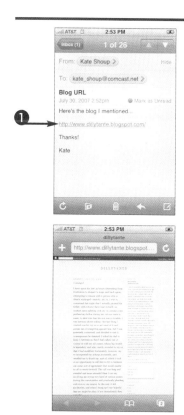

**1** With the message containing the link open in your iPhone, tap the link.

iPhone launches the necessary application to display the contents of the link.

In addition to receiving e-mail messages through your iPhone, you can send them. One way to send a message is to reply to a message that you have received.

If the message to which you are replying was sent to multiple people, you can choose to send your reply to everyone on the list, or only to the sender.

In addition to replying to a message, you can also forward a message to a third party. For example, you might choose to forward a message from your boss to the other employees on your team. When you forward a message, you can also add your own text to the message.

① With the message to which you want to reply open, tap **Reply** (⤺).

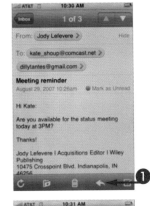

② Choose the desired option.

• You can tap **Reply** to reply only to the sender.

• If you are one of multiple recipients, you can tap **Reply All** to reply to the sender and to all other recipients.

• To forward the message to a third party, you can tap **Forward**.

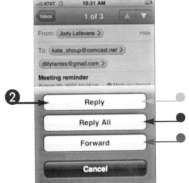

**3** Type your message with the keyboard that appears.

**4** Tap **Send**.

iPhone sends the message.

● Sent messages are listed in the Sent folder.

**Did You Know?**

You can add the sender of an e-mail or any additional recipients to your list of contacts. To do so, tap the e-mail message in your Inbox and, if necessary, tap **Details** to display all of the recipients. Then tap the entry for the sender or for the recipient that you want to add to your contacts list, and tap **Create New Contact**. Enter any additional information that you have about the contact and then tap **Save**.

You can start your own thread of messages by creating a new message.

As you begin typing a contact's name or e-mail address in the To or CC field, your iPhone displays a list of contacts that match what you have typed, enabling you to select the one you want. If the intended recipient has not been added to your contacts list, you can simply type the recipient's e-mail address.

Unfortunately, the iPhone does not offer the Blind Carbon Copy, or BCC, feature.

① Tap **Mail** (▨) on the main iPhone screen.

② Tap **New E-mail Message** (▨).

**Note:** If you have set up your iPhone to manage multiple e-mail accounts, you may need to first tap the account whose Inbox you want to view.

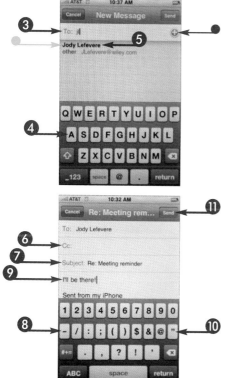

③ Tap the **To** field.

④ Type the name or e-mail address of the intended recipient.

● iPhone displays a list of contacts that match what you typed.

⑤ Tap the desired contact in the list.

● You can also tap (🔵) to display the All Contacts screen, from which you can select the desired contact.

⑥ Tap the **To** field or the **CC** field and then repeat steps **5** and **6** to add more recipients.

⑦ Tap the **Subject** field.

⑧ Type a subject for the message.

⑨ Tap the body of the message.

⑩ Type your message.

⑪ Tap **Send**.

The message is sent.

**Try This!**

By default, all outgoing e-mail messages contain an e-mail signature that reads, "Sent from my iPhone." You can change this signature or remove it. To do so, tap **Settings** (🔵) on the main iPhone screen, tap **Mail**, and tap **Signature**. Then use the keyboard that appears to either delete the existing signature or replace it with new text.

# Save an E-Mail Message as a Draft

Suppose you are composing an e-mail message but you run out of time to finish it. Rather than sending it off before it is ready, or losing what you have written so far, you can save the message as a *draft*. When you are ready to resume writing, you can re-open the message and start where you left off.

When you save a message as a draft, your iPhone creates a Drafts folder and saves the unfinished message there; when you resume writing the message, you can access it from within this folder.

---

① With the message you want to save as a draft open, tap **Cancel**.

***Note:*** *For help creating and composing a message, see the section, "Compose and Send a New E-Mail Message."*

② Tap **Save**.

● If this is the first time you have saved a draft, the iPhone creates a Drafts folder, placing the message inside it.

③ To open the saved message, tap **Drafts**.

● A list appears of messages that are saved as drafts.

④ Tap the message you want to finish to open it.

**TIP**

**Remove It!**

If you compose a message but decide not to send it, you can delete it instead of saving it as a draft. To delete the message, tap **Cancel**, and tap **Don't Save**. Your iPhone cancels the message. To delete a message from within the Drafts folder, tap the **Edit** button, tap ⊖ next to the message you want to delete, and then tap the **Delete** button that appears.

When someone sends you a text message, the message appears on the main iPhone screen, even if your iPhone is locked. Buttons that enable you to either ignore or view the message also appear.

You can ignore the message, accessing it later by tapping the Text button in the main iPhone screen. The Text Message screen appears, listing text messages and grouping them into conversations;

conversations containing unread messages are marked with a blue dot. Tap the conversation that contains the new message to view it in full.

To prevent text messages from being displayed automatically upon receipt, tap the Settings button on the main screen, tap General, tap Passcode Lock, and toggle the Show SMS Preview setting off.

---

When you receive a new text message, it appears in the main iPhone screen.

① To view the message, drag the slider at the bottom of the screen.

**Note:** If the iPhone is not in sleep mode, the text message will simply appear on the iPhone screen; touch the message to view it in full.

● The complete contents of the message display.

Unless they have been deleted, earlier messages from the sender also display.

If you are in range of your cell network, you can easily reply to a text message.

In addition to replying to a text message by texting your response, you can also reply by calling or e-mailing the sender if the sender's e-mail address and phone number have been saved in your contacts list.

To call the person who sent you the text message, you can tap the Call button at the top of the message screen. To e-mail them, you can tap the Contact Info button at the top of the message screen and then tap the contact's e-mail address.

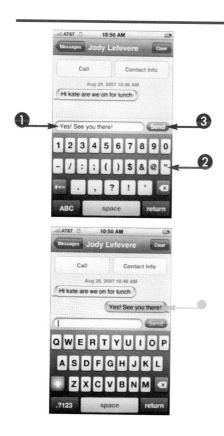

➊ Tap the field at the bottom of the text message to which you want to respond.

The iPhone keyboard appears.

➋ Type your reply.

➌ Tap **Send**.

The iPhone sends your reply.

● Your response appears along the right side of the screen.

You are not limited to replying to text messages that you receive from others. You can also start your own conversations. You can do so from within the Text Messages screen, which you access by tapping the Text button on the main iPhone screen.

You can only start a new conversation with a contact if old conversations with that person have been deleted. Otherwise, the message that you enter is simply appended to the end of the existing conversation. If you want to start a new conversation, make sure to delete the old conversation with your contact.

---

① In the Text Messages screen, tap **New Text Message** ( ).

The New Message screen appears.

② Tap the **To** field.

③ Begin typing the name or phone number of the intended recipient.

● Your iPhone displays a list of contacts that match what you typed.

④ Tap the desired contact in the list.

● You can also tap to display the All Contacts screen, from which you can select the desired contact.

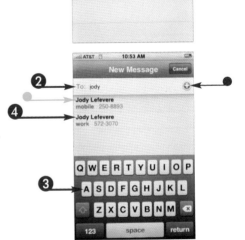

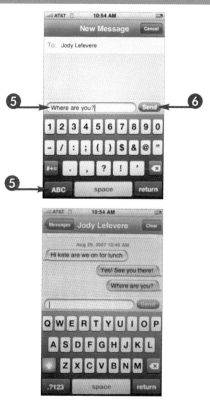

⑤ Type your message.

⑥ Tap **Send**.

The iPhone sends your text message.

### More Options!

Another way to create a message is by tapping **Text Message** in the Info screen of a contact. If multiple phone numbers have been entered in the contact's record, you are prompted to select the one to which you want to send the message; you can then type your message and tap **Send**.

# Enjoying Audio Content on Your iPhone

You can use your iPhone to listen to music and other audio content such as podcasts. To do this, you must sync your iPhone with iTunes; when you do, audio content that you select is automatically copied to the iPhone.

Before syncing, you must import your audio content into iTunes. One way to do

this is to purchase content online from the iTunes Store or obtain it from other Internet sources. Another way is to rip it from CDs.

You can group audio content in iTunes into playlists, or compilations. For example, you may want to create a playlist for songs you like to listen to as you exercise. You can then add those playlist to your iPhone.

# Quick Tips

You can copy the audio content that is stored on your computer to your iPhone. You do this through a sync operation. New content that you add to iTunes is ported to your iPhone the next time you sync.

If your computer holds more audio content than your iPhone can store, you can choose to sync only certain playlists. This allows you to limit the content that is copied to your iPhone. One approach is to create an iTunes playlist that contains only the content you want to add to your iPhone. In addition to syncing music, you can also sync podcasts and audio books to your iPhone.

---

① Connect your iPhone to your computer.

② Click the entry for your iPhone in the iTunes Source list.

③ Click the **Music** tab.

***Note:*** *To sync podcasts, click the **Podcasts** tab, click the **Sync** check box, and then click the podcasts that you want to sync.*

④ Click **Sync music** (☐ changes to ☑).

● Click here to copy all audio content onto your iPhone.

● Click here to copy only selected playlists.

● If you are copying only selected playlists, click the check box next to each desired playlist.

***Note:*** *To sync audio books, select the **Audiobooks** check box.*

⑤ Click **Apply**.

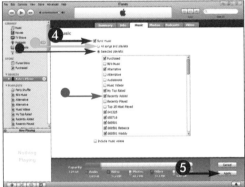

One way to adjust volume on your iPhone is to drag the volume slider that appears at the bottom of the screen when you play a song; moving to the left decreases volume, while moving to the right increases it. Alternatively, you can press the volume buttons on the left side of the iPhone to adjust the playback volume.

While adjusting volume using either of these approaches changes the volume for files that are playing, it does not compensate for when certain songs have been recorded at different levels, making them louder or softer. You can set up your iPhone to play all of your media files at the same volume level by using the Sound Check feature.

① In the Settings screen, tap **iPod**.

*Note:* To access the Settings screen, tap **Settings** (⚙) in the main iPhone screen.

The iPod screen appears.

② In the Sound Check field, tap **Off**.

Off toggles to On, enabling the Sound Check option.

③ Press the **Home** button to change the setting and return to the main iPhone screen.

You can use the iPhone EQ function to fine-tune your sound. The EQ function includes more than 20 pre-set configurations from which to choose, many designed for specific genres. For example, you may frequently listen to a particular type of music, such as classical. In this case, you can choose the Classical EQ setting to ensure that your favorite music is played back using the best possible EQ configuration. Other genre-based pre-sets include Acoustic, Dance, Electronic, Hip Hop, Lounge, Pop, and Rock.

In addition to choosing genre-based EQ configurations, you can also choose from pre-sets such as Bass Booster, Bass Reducer, Treble Booster, Treble Reducer, and Vocal Booster. There is even a Small Speaker EQ pre-set, designed to enhance playback on smaller speakers.

---

① In the iPod screen, tap **EQ**.

***Note:*** *To access the iPod screen, tap **Settings** (⚙) in the main iPhone screen and then tap **iPod** in the Settings screen.*

The EQ screen appears.

② Tap the EQ pre-set you want to use.

● A check mark appears next to the selected pre-set.

③ Press the **Home** button to confirm the setting change and return to the main iPhone screen.

If you play audio content on your iPhone at a high volume, you can damage your hearing. To protect your ears, you can set a volume limit. This ensures that even when the slider and volume buttons are at their maximum settings, your iPhone is not so loud as to cause damage. This volume limit applies only when a headset, headphones, or speakers are connected to your iPhone.

You can also lock in the volume limit, preventing others from changing it. Only people who know this code can change the volume limit you set.

① In the iPod screen, tap **Volume Limit**.

**Note:** To access the iPod screen, tap **Settings** (⚙) in the main iPhone screen and tap **iPod** in the Settings screen.

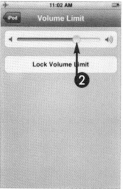

The Volume Limit screen appears.

② Drag the Volume Limit slider to decrease or increase the volume limit.

If you are currently playing music, the audio adjusts to reflect the volume limit you set.

③ Press the **Home** button to confirm the setting change and return to the main iPhone screen.

Although it is great to be able to store over 7GB of content on your iPhone, it can also be difficult to find the audio file you want to play.

Fortunately, the iPhone is designed to help you easily find the content you want, by providing an intuitive menu system that sorts audio content in a variety of ways. One way is to sort your audio content alphabetically by song. You can also sort by artist, album, composer, genre, or playlist.

If you choose one of these alternative sorting methods, you can locate a song by tapping the name of the song's artist, album, composer, genre, or playlist, and then scroll through the list of songs that appears.

① In the main iPhone screen, tap **iPod** ( ).

The iPod screen appears.

● You can tap **Playlists** to view a list of playlists on your iPhone.

● You can tap **Artists** to sort your audio content by artist.

● You can tap **Songs** to view a list of songs, as shown in this example.

● You can tap **More** to access options that enable you to sort audio content by album, composer, or genre, or to listen to audio books or podcasts.

After you locate a song, playing it is as simple as tapping it on your iPhone. Although the iPhone does have a speaker that enables you to hear the song directly from the device, you can enjoy a superior audio experience using the stereo headphones that came with your iPhone.

By default, your iPhone plays songs alphabetically, except in the case of playlists. You can use playlists to play the songs you want, in the order you specify. You can also choose to play songs in shuffle mode, which is in random order. To do this, you can use the Shuffle button that appears at the top of the list of songs.

① Locate and tap the song you want to play.

Your iPhone plays the song.

● You can tap here to pause playback.

● You can tap and drag the slider to adjust playback volume.

● You can tap here to restart the current song or to hear the song that precedes it in the list.

● You can tap here to jump to the next song.

You can use your iPhone to create a playlist on the go — that is, when the device is not connected to iTunes — by adding songs to its special On-The-Go playlist. This will enable you to listen to your favorite songs while on the go. You can access the On-The-Go playlist by tapping the iPod button on the main iPhone screen, tapping Playlists in the screen that appears, and then tapping On-The-Go.

Because space can become limited on your iPhone over time, you may not want to leave a song on your On-The-Go playlist forever. The On-The-Go screen enables you to remove a song, or remove an entire playlist.

---

**①** Tap **iPod** (  ) in the main iPhone screen.

**②** Tap **Playlists** (  ).

**③** Tap **On-The-Go**.

If this is the first time you are adding songs to your On-The-Go playlist, you are prompted to select the songs you want to add.

④ Tap a song to add it to the list.

The song you tap appears grayed out.

⑤ Repeat step **4** until you have added all of the songs you want.

⑥ Tap **Done**.

● The songs you selected are added to the On-The-Go playlist.

### Did You Know?

To add more songs to the list later, tap the **Edit** button, and then tap ▦ in the upper-left corner of the On-The-Go screen. In the Songs screen, tap a song to add it to the list. After you finish adding songs, tap **Done**.

A *podcast* is a pre-recorded digital media file that typically contains an episode of a radio- or television-style show. You can download podcast episodes from the iTunes Store or from other online sources. Podcasts are usually free of charge.

If you really like a podcast, you can *subscribe* to it. When you subscribe to a podcast, files for new episodes are downloaded automatically to iTunes. You can copy podcast episodes to your iPhone by syncing it with iTunes.

Although the iTunes Store offers a great selection of podcasts, this only represents a small number of the podcasts available worldwide. To locate podcasts not offered through the iTunes Store, you can visit a podcast directory, such as allpodcasts.com, ipodder.org, and podcastalley.com.

① Tap **iPod** ( ) on the main iPhone screen.

② Tap **More**.

③ Tap **Podcasts**.

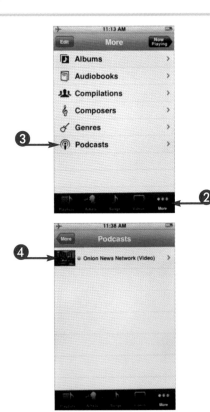

The Podcasts screen appears, displaying a list of podcasts on your iPhone.

④ Tap the podcast you want to hear.

A list of episodes appears for the selected podcast.

⑤ Tap the episode you want to play.

Your iPhone plays the podcast.

**Important!**

You can copy podcast episodes to your iPhone by syncing it with iTunes. To do so, connect your iPhone to your computer, click the entry for the iPhone in the Source list, and then click the **Podcasts** tab. Select the **Sync** check box, choose which podcasts you want to sync, click **Apply**, and if necessary, click **Sync**.

You can use your iPhone to listen to audio books, which you can purchase at the iTunes Store. After you purchase and download an audio book from the iTunes Store to your computer, you can make it available on your iPhone by syncing the device.

You can also import audio books on CD into iTunes. Audio books that you import

in this manner do not appear under Audiobooks in the iTunes Source list or the iPhone menu structure. Instead, they appear as files in your music library.

*Note: Sharing audio books copied from CD, and failing to delete them after listening to them, is a violation of the audio book's copyright.*

① Tap **iPod** ( ) on the main iPhone screen.

② Tap **More**.

③ Tap **Audiobooks**.

The Audiobooks screen appears, displaying a list of audio books on your iPod.

**Note:** *If the audio book you want to listen to was imported from a CD, it does not appear under Audiobooks in the iPhone menu structure. Instead, it is simply listed among the files in your music library.*

④ Tap the audio book you want to hear.

If the audio book has been divided into parts or chapters, a list of them appears here.

⑤ Tap the part you want to hear.

Your iPhone plays the audio book.

**Note:** *If you do not like the speed at which an audio book is read, you can change it. To do so, tap **Settings** (⚙) in the main iPhone screen, tap **iPod**, tap **Audiobook Speed**, and tap **Slower**, **Normal**, or **Faster**.*

**Important!**
You can copy audio books in your iTunes library to your iPhone by syncing your iPhone with iTunes. To do so, first connect your iPhone to your computer, click the entry for your iPhone in the iTunes Source list, and click the **Music** tab. If you choose to sync all songs and playlists, audio books are synced automatically. If you choose to sync selected playlists only, select the **Audiobooks** check box under Selected Playlists.

If you have purchased a song on iTunes, you may be able to convert it for use as a ringtone with the iPhone mobile phone feature. Note that to use a song as a ringtone, you must pay a $1 fee — this is in addition to the original fee you paid to purchase the song from iTunes. Songs that can be used as ringtones are marked in iTunes by a small icon that looks like a bell.

During the conversion process, you can specify which part of the song should comprise the ringtone, the duration of the part featured (up to 30 seconds), the duration of the gap between each playback iteration, and whether the selected part should fade in and out.

① In iTunes, click **Purchased** in the source list.

② Click the song you want to convert to a ringtone.

③ Click **Store**.

④ Click **Create Ringtone**.

If you are not currently logged in to the iTunes Store, an iTunes dialog box appears.

⑤ Type your Apple ID.

⑥ Type your password.

⑦ Click **Buy**.

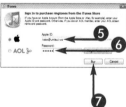

A pane appears at the bottom of the screen.

**8** Click and drag the blue area to specify which portion of the song should constitute the ringtone.

● Use the **Fade In** and **Fade Out** check boxes to specify whether the ringtone fades in and out.

**9** Click the **Looping** and specify how long the gap between each playback iteration should be.

**10** Click **Preview** to preview the clip.

**11** When you are satisfied with the clip, click **Buy**.

The ringtone is created and placed in the source list's Ringtones folder.

### Important!

To copy the ringtone to your iPhone, perform a sync. Connect the iPhone to your computer, click **iPhone** in the iTunes source list, click the **Ringtones** tab in the screen that appears, specify whether you want to sync all ringtones or only the ones you select, and click **Apply**. After the ringtone is copied over, you select it for use with your iPhone just as you would any other ringtone.

# Enjoying Video Content on Your iPhone

Among the many features of iPhone, its capability to play video is perhaps its most notable. Thanks to its storage capacity and crystal-clear screen, your iPhone is ideal for enjoying video content, from amateur-produced clips found on the Internet to full-length studio-released feature films.

One way to obtain video for your iPhone is by purchasing it from the iTunes Store. There you can find episodes of television shows, music videos, short films, and feature-length movies, all available for download. In addition, you can download movie trailers and video podcasts from the iTunes Store free of charge.

You can also download video from other online sources, such as Google Video. After you download a video onto your computer, you can import it into iTunes. After video content has been downloaded or imported into iTunes, you can sync your iPhone with iTunes to copy it to your iPhone.

In addition to viewing video content that you have synced from iTunes, you can also use your iPhone to access video content directly from YouTube, a popular video-sharing Web site where you can view video clips.

# Quick Tips

# Optimize a Video for Viewing on Your iPhone

Before you can use your iPhone to watch a video, you may need to optimize the video for playback on your iPhone, especially if the video was imported into iTunes instead of purchased directly from the iTunes Store. The optimization process can take several minutes — longer if the file is particularly large or your computer is particularly slow. A copy of

the un-optimized version of the video remains in your iTunes library.

After you have optimized a video, you can port it to your iPhone just as you would any other type of content by syncing the iPhone with iTunes. For more information about syncing video to your iPhone, see the section, "Sync Video Content."

① In iTunes, locate and select the video you want to optimize.

② Click **Advanced**.

③ Click **Convert Selection for iPod**.

● iTunes creates a copy of the file, optimizing it for playback on your iPhone.

You can copy a video that is stored on your computer to your iPhone using a sync operation. iTunes divides video content into a few different categories. One category is movies, a second is TV shows, and a third is video podcasts. TV shows and movies are synced from the Video tab of the iPhone sync interface; music videos are synced from the Music tab; and video podcasts are synced from the Podcasts tab.

Although iTunes does not differentiate between video podcasts and audio podcasts in the iPhone sync interface, the iPhone does differentiate between these two types of podcasts. Note that when syncing TV shows, you can sync all episodes of a show or selected episodes only.

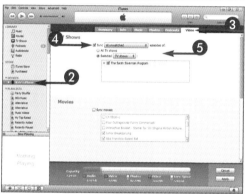

1. Connect your iPhone to your computer.

2. Click the iPhone entry in the iTunes Source list.

3. Click **Video**.

4. Under TV Shows, click **Sync** (☐ changes to ☑).

5. Click the necessary options to specify which episodes you want to sync.

6. Click **Sync movies** (☐ changes to ☑).

7. Click the movies you want to copy to your iPhone (☐ changes to ☑).

8. Click **Apply**.

# Browse Video Content

After you sync video content to your iPhone, you can use your iPhone to watch it. Your iPhone sorts video content into a few categories: movies, TV shows, music videos, and podcasts. All video categories display in the Videos screen. If you have a lot of video content on your iPhone, you may need to scroll down to see it all.

Although most iPhones offer more than 7GB of storage, video files can quickly consume this space. For this reason, iPhone makes it easy to delete videos. One way to delete a video is to locate it in the Videos screen, drag your finger across it from left to right, and tap the Delete button that appears.

① In the main iPhone screen, tap **iPod** ( ).

The iPod screen appears.

② Tap **Videos**.

The iPhone displays a list of videos stored on your device, sorted under the headings Movies, TV Shows, Music Videos, and Podcasts.

You can use your iPhone to watch movies that you purchase from the iTunes Store or that you import into iTunes from your computer. Your iPhone plays movies and other video content in widescreen mode, meaning that you must turn your iPhone sideways to view it properly.

If you want to watch a music video instead of a movie, simply locate the video you want to watch under the Music

Videos heading instead of the Movies heading. After you watch a movie, the iPhone asks whether you want to delete it. Note that if you delete the movie, iTunes will try to re-add it the next time you sync unless you deselect the check box next to the movie in the Sync screen's Video tab.

① In the main iPhone screen, tap **iPod** (▣).

② Tap **Videos**.

Movies are listed under the Movies heading, at the top of the screen.

③ Tap the movie you want to watch.

④ To view playback controls, tap anywhere on the screen.

● You can tap here to play or pause the video.

● You can drag the slider to adjust the volume.

● You can drag the scrubber to move forward or backward through the video.

● You can tap here to scale the video to make it fill the screen.

A *podcast* is a digital media file that is distributed over the Internet. Although most podcasts are audio files, video podcasts are gaining in popularity.

Typically, a video podcast contains an episode of a television-style show. You can download video podcast episodes from the iTunes Store, or from other online sources.

If you like a video podcast, you can subscribe to it. When you do this, iTunes automatically downloads new episodes.

You copy video podcasts from iTunes to your iPhone by syncing the device. You specify which podcasts should be synced from the Podcasts tab in the iTunes sync interface.

Although iTunes does not differentiate between video and audio podcasts in the iPhone sync interface, the iPhone does differentiate between these two types of podcasts.

1 In the main iPhone screen, tap **iPod** (📱).

The iPod screen appears.

2 Tap **Videos**.

3 Tap the video podcast you want to watch.

A list of episodes appears for the selected video podcast.

**4** Tap the episode you want to watch.

Your iPhone plays the video podcast.

**5** To view the playback controls, tap anywhere on the screen.

***Note:*** *For more information on the playback controls, see the section, "Watch a Movie on Your iPhone."*

### Check It Out!

While the iTunes Store offers a great selection of video podcasts, this is only a small number of the video podcasts that are available worldwide. To locate video podcasts not offered through the iTunes Store, try visiting a podcast directory, such as http://videopodcasts.tv.

If you missed an episode of your favorite TV show, you may be able to purchase it from the iTunes Store. In addition to purchasing single episodes of shows, you can also purchase Season Passes or Multi-Passes.

A *Season Pass* enables you to purchase an entire season of a program that is ongoing. A *Multi-Pass* allows you to buy a set number of episodes. A third option, *Buy Season*, enables you to purchase all of the episodes of a season that has already aired in its entirety.

You can copy TV episodes from iTunes that you have downloaded to your iPhone. For more information, see the section "Sync Video Content."

---

① In the main iPhone screen, tap **iPod** ( ).

The iPod screen appears.

② Tap **Videos**.

③ Tap the TV show you want to watch.

*Note: You may need to scroll down to locate the show; they are listed under the heading TV Shows.*

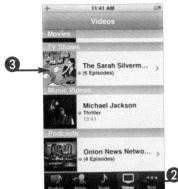

A list of episodes appears for the selected TV show.

④ Tap the episode you want to watch.

Your iPhone plays the TV show episode.

⑤ To view the playback controls, tap anywhere on the screen.

*Note:* For more information on the playback controls, see the section, "Watch a Movie on Your iPhone."

**Did You Know?**

The Playlists, Artists, Songs, and Videos buttons display along the bottom of the iPhone screen in iPod mode. If you frequently access other content — say, audiobooks — you can replace one of the default buttons with the Audiobooks button. To do so, tap the **More** button, tap **Edit**, and drag the new button to the bottom of the screen, over the button you want to replace. Then, tap **Done**.

# View Featured Videos on YouTube

Your iPhone provides direct access to YouTube, a popular video-sharing Web site where you can view video clips. Some clips are created by amateur filmmakers; others are posted to the site by television networks such as CBS; still others are music videos, such as those provided by Universal Music Group and Sony BMG Music Entertainment.

The sheer volume of content on YouTube can make it difficult to find videos of interest. For this reason, the YouTube staff reviews some videos, placing those that it deems interesting in the Featured category of the site. You can easily access videos in this category with your iPhone.

① Tap **YouTube** (▣) on the main iPhone screen.

② Tap a video in the list to view it.

The video plays.

● When the video is over, your iPhone displays information about it, such as its rating, description, and date added.

● A list of similar videos also appears.

---

**Important!**

You can access playback controls for YouTube videos the same way you access the controls for regular videos: by tapping the screen during playback. These controls include a Play/Pause button, a Rewind button, a Fast-Forward button, and a scrubber that enables you to drag forward or backward through a video.

# Locate Most-Viewed Videos on YouTube

According to Nielsen/NetRatings, YouTube receives more than 20 million visitors each month. The Web site offers 100 million clips, with 65,000 more added every 24 hours. You can use your iPhone to sort them by Most Viewed. This enables you to keep up with current trends by watching videos that others around the world are enjoying most frequently.

Most Viewed videos are divided into three categories: all-time most viewed, most viewed today, and most viewed this week.

In addition to sorting videos on YouTube by Most Viewed, you can also display them by using the following categories: Top Rated, Most Recent, and History.

① Tap **YouTube** (📺) on the main iPhone screen.

② Tap **Most Viewed**.

● A list appears of all-time most-viewed videos.

③ Tap **Today**.

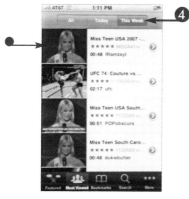

● A list appears of today's most-viewed videos.

④ Tap **This Week**.

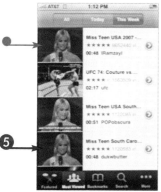

● A list appears of this week's most-viewed videos.

⑤ Tap a video to watch it.

Your iPhone plays the video.

**More Options!**

To sort YouTube videos by Top Rated, Most Recent, or History, tap the **More** button, and then tap the desired option in the screen that appears. To allow for quicker sorting by these parameters, tap the **Edit** button in the More screen and drag the **Top Rated**, **Most Recent**, or **History** button to the bottom of the screen, over the button you want to replace. Then, tap **Done**.

# Search for Videos on YouTube

YouTube boasts an enormous quantity of content — more than 100 million clips, with 65,000 more added every 24 hours, with videos ranging from amateur-produced clips to content from television networks such as CBS.

As wonderful as it is to have so much content available, it can make it difficult to find a particular video. Fortunately, the YouTube feature on your iPhone offers a search function, which you can use to locate clips. Simply use the iPhone intelligent keyboard to type a keyword, and let YouTube locate the clip you want. Possible keywords include video titles, tags, usernames, and descriptions.

① Tap **YouTube** ( ) on the main iPhone screen.

② Tap **Search** ( ).

③ Tap the empty search field at the top of the screen.

The iPhone intelligent keyboard appears.

④ Type a keyword.

⑤ Tap **Search**.

Your iPhone returns a list of videos that relate to the keyword you typed.

⑥ Tap a video to play it.

**More Options!**

To see more information about a video listed in the search results, or in the Featured or Most Viewed screen, tap 📄 next to the video. This reveals the title, rating, and duration of the video, as well as a description of the clip, the date it was added, its category, and any tags associated with the clip.

# Bookmark a Video on YouTube

If you find a video that you really like, you can *bookmark* it. Bookmarking a video is like marking it as a favorite.

You can bookmark a video in one of two ways. The first way is to tap the Bookmark button as the video plays. The second way is to bookmark a video from the information screen that YouTube displays after the video has played. You can also access the information screen by tapping the right-arrow button next to the video in the Featured, Most Viewed, Most Recent, Top Rated, or History list, or in a list of search results.

If you decide you no longer want to bookmark a video, you can easily remove it from the list of bookmarked clips.

## BOOKMARK A VIDEO

**1** After you locate the video that you want to bookmark on YouTube, tap next to the video.

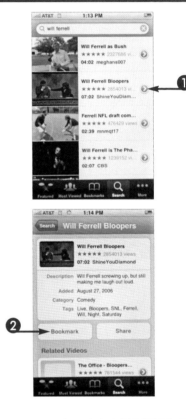

Your iPhone displays the information screen for the video.

***Note:*** *Another option is to watch the video you want to bookmark; when the video ends, the information screen is displayed by default.*

**2** Tap **Bookmark**.

Your iPhone adds the video to your list of bookmarked clips.

**LOCATE BOOKMARKED CLIPS**

① Tap **Bookmarks** ().

Your iPhone displays a list of bookmarked clips.

② To view a bookmarked clip, tap it in the list.

Your iPhone plays the clip.

---

**TIP**

**Remove It!**

If you no longer want to bookmark a video, you can remove it from your list of bookmarked clips. To do so, tap the **Edit** button in the Bookmarks screen, tap 🔴 next to the clip you want to remove, and then tap the **Delete** button.

You may encounter a video on YouTube that you absolutely must share with others. To make this easier, the iPhone allows you to e-mail links to YouTube videos with the tap of a button.

You can e-mail a video link in one of two ways. The first way is to tap the Send button as the video plays. The second way is to send a video link from the

information screen that YouTube displays after the video has played.

You can also access this information screen by tapping the right-arrow button next to the video in the Featured, Most Viewed, Most Recent, Top Rated, or History list, or in a list of search results.

---

**1** Tap **YouTube** ( ) on the main iPhone screen.

**2** Locate the video you want to e-mail, and tap .

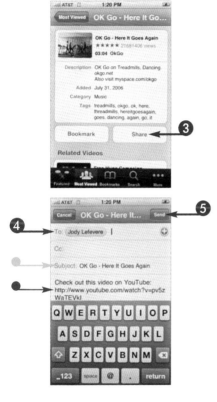

Your iPhone displays the information screen for the video.

③ Tap **Share**.

The iPhone intelligent keyboard appears.

④ Tap the **To** field and type the name or e-mail address for the person with whom you want to share the video.

● You can tap the **Subject** field and type a subject for the message.

● You can tap the body of the message and type a message for the recipient.

⑤ Tap **Send**.

Your iPhone sends the link.

**Did You Know?**

As you type the recipient's name or e-mail address in the To field, iPhone displays a list of contacts that match what you typed. Tap the desired contact in the list. Alternatively, tap the ⊕ to display the All Contacts screen, from which you can select the desired contact. If the recipient has not yet been entered in your Contacts list, you must type the addressee's e-mail address manually.

# Using Your iPhone to Take and Share Photos

If you store digital photographs on your computer, you can copy them to your iPhone. In addition, you can use the 2-megapixel camera that is built into your iPhone to take pictures while on the go. You can also export images captured with the iPhone camera feature back to your computer.

The iPhone sorts your photos into albums — both those taken with the iPhone camera feature and those synced from your computer. When you open an iPhone album, photos in that album display in contact-sheet format — that is, they appear in a small thumbnail format. You can view these thumbnail images in a larger format, zooming in to specific areas of an image or rotating it from a vertical orientation to a horizontal one, and vice versa.

You can generate a slide show using photos stored on your iPhone. You establish the settings for the show using the iPhone Settings screen. For example, you can specify how long each image displays, whether images should be repeated or shuffled, and what type of transition effect should be used when switching from one image to the next. You can also e-mail photos stored on your iPhone to others.

# Quick Tips

If you store digital photographs on your computer, you can copy them to your iPhone. You can choose whether all photos are copied, or only the photos within a particular folder on your computer's hard drive.

If you use a Mac, you can use the iLife suite, which contains both iTunes and

iPhoto. Apple has integrated the iLife suite so well that, where appropriate, the applications can use each other's data. This means that iTunes can work with graphic files and photo albums stored in iPhoto libraries; as a result, you can copy photos and albums — including smart albums — onto your iPhone.

---

**①** Connect your iPhone to your computer.

**②** Click the entry for your iPhone in the iTunes Source list.

**③** Click the **Photos** tab.

**④** Click **Sync photos from** (☐ changes to ☑).

**⑤** Click the **Sync photos from** ⬍ and select the folder that contains the photos you want to copy to your iPhone.

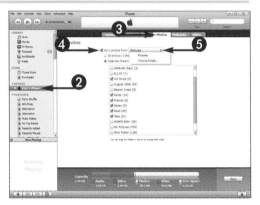

● You can click here to copy all photos in the selected folder to your iPhone.

● You can click here to copy only photos that are stored in certain subfolders or albums.

● You can click the applicable folder to include photos in selected folders or albums.

**⑥** Click **Apply**.

iTunes copies the photos to your iPhone.

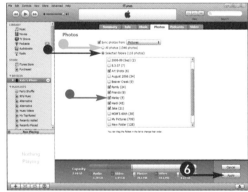

Your iPhone features a built-in 2-megapixel camera that you can use to snap digital photos while on the go. Although the photos you take with your iPhone will not be of the same quality as those taken with many dedicated digital cameras, they are often superior to those taken with traditional cell-phone cameras. Unfortunately, the iPhone camera does not offer flash functionality.

The lens for the iPhone camera is located on the back of the iPhone, allowing you to preview the scene you are about to photograph on the iPhone screen. You can take photos holding your iPhone vertically, in *portrait mode*, or rotated horizontally, in *landscape mode*.

① Tap **Camera** (📷) on the main iPhone screen.

The iPhone camera screen appears.

② Point the backside of the iPhone at the scene you want to photograph.

● The scene appears on the iPhone screen.

③ Tap **Camera** (📷).

Your iPhone photographs the scene.

Your iPhone sorts your photos into various albums. For example, Camera Roll stores photos taken with the iPhone camera feature, and Photo Library contains all photos that you have copied to your iPhone from your computer. Any other folders or albums that you copy from your computer to your iPhone appear as separate albums.

When you open an iPhone album, photos in that album display in contact-sheet, or thumbnail, format. To view a specific photo in a larger format, you can simply tap it. Once a photo displays in this larger format, you can skip to the next or previous photo in the album with the tap of a button, or return to the album to select another photo.

① On the main iPhone screen, tap **Photos** (📷).

The Photo Albums screen appears.

② Tap the album that contains the photo you want to view.

The photos in the selected album appear in contact-sheet format.

③ Tap the photo you want to view.

● You can tap here to return to the previous photo in the album.

● You can tap here to move to the next photo.

**Note:** *You can also move forward or backward through the album by flicking — dragging your finger across the current photo from left to right or right to left.*

● You can tap here to start a slide show of photos in the selected album.

**More Options!**

Another way to access photos taken with the iPhone camera is to tap the **Camera** button (📷) on the main iPhone screen, and then tap the **View Photos** button (▣) in the bottom-left corner of the screen. After you view photos taken with the camera, you can switch to the camera function by tapping ▣ again.

To get a better look at a photo, you can zoom in to see it close up, or zoom out to take a long view. One way to zoom in is to double-tap the part of the image you want to view up close. You can also reverse pinch the picture — starting with your thumb and index finger pinched together, and then spreading them apart.

If you can no longer see the portion of the image that you want to view when you zoom in, you can pan around the photo by dragging your finger over the image.

To zoom back out, double-tap the image again, or pinch the photo, this time starting with your fingers spread apart and then pinching them together.

① Double-tap the spot on the picture you want to view more closely.

The image enlarges to the spot you tapped.

If you shot an image horizontally, in landscape mode, viewing it with your iPhone positioned vertically, in portrait mode, may not do it justice. Instead, you can view it with the iPhone positioned horizontally; that way, the image consumes the entire screen, and appears larger.

When you view a photo horizontally, in landscape mode, you can still zoom in and out, or move to the next or previous photos in the album by dragging. You can also tap the screen to display the controls, although the controls remain in the same place as when photos display in portrait mode.

① With the iPhone positioned vertically, in portrait mode, rotate it 90 degrees to the left or right.

The image on the screen rotates accordingly, now appearing in landscape mode.

*Note:* To return to portrait mode, you can rotate the iPhone back to the vertical position.

You can use your iPhone to generate a photo slide show. To do this, you must first establish the slide show settings. For example, you can choose how long each image displays, whether images should repeat or be shuffled, and what type of transition effect, if any, should be used when switching from one image to the next. You can also choose to play the songs in a particular playlist during the slide show.

After you establish these settings, you can run a slide show of a particular album or folder. You simply select the album or folder in the iPhone Photo Albums screen and then tap the Play button at the bottom of the screen that displays the album images in thumbnail format.

① In the iPhone Settings screen, tap **Photos**.

***Note:*** *To access the iPhone Settings screen, tap **Settings** (⚙) in the main iPhone screen.*

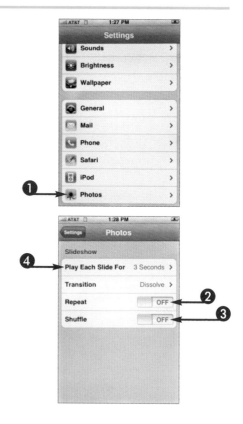

The Photos screen appears.

② To repeat a slide show, tap **Off** next to Repeat.

The Repeat option toggles from Off to On.

③ To arrange the photos in random order, tap **Off** next to Shuffle.

The Shuffle option toggles from Off to On.

④ Tap **Play Each Slide For**.

The Play Each Slide For screen appears.

**5** Tap the desired duration.

**6** Tap **Photos** to return to the Photos screen.

**7** In the Photos screen, tap **Transition** (see the previous screen).

The Transition screen appears.

**8** Tap the desired transition type.

**9** Press the **Home** button to confirm the setting and return to the main iPhone screen.

### Try This!

Almost any photo slide show can be enhanced by a musical accompaniment. To play your slide show with music in the background, simply tap the **iPod** button (📱) in the main iPhone screen, locate the song you want to hear in the background during the slide show, and play it.

Whether you take a photograph using your iPhone camera or you sync a digital image from your computer, you can easily e-mail any photo stored on your iPhone to others.

When you choose to e-mail a picture, the iPhone creates a new e-mail message and displays its intelligent keyboard; you simply enter the necessary contact

information, a subject for your e-mail, and any message text you want to include.

If your iPhone is set up to use multiple e-mail accounts, the default one is used to send photos. If you want to use a different account, you must set it as the default. For more information on setting the default e-mail account, see Chapter 5.

① With the picture you want to e-mail displayed on the iPhone screen, tap 📧.

**Note:** If 📧 is not displayed, tap anywhere on the photo to reveal it.

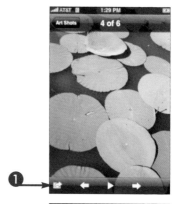

② Tap **Email Photo**.

Your iPhone creates a new e-mail message containing the photo.

③ Tap the **To** field.

The intelligent keyboard appears.

④ Type the name or e-mail address for the person with whom you want to share the photo.

● You can tap the **Subject** field and type a subject for the message.

● You can tap the body of the message and type a message for the recipient.

⑤ Tap **Send**.

**Attention!**

As you type the recipient's name or e-mail address in the To field, iPhone displays a list of contacts that match what you typed; tap the desired contact in the list. You can also tap ⊕ to display the All Contacts screen, from which you can select the desired contact. If the recipient has not yet been entered in your Contacts list, you must type the addressee's e-mail address manually.

You can copy photos taken with the iPhone camera feature to your computer. For example, you might want to have a print made of the photo using an online photo service such as Shutterfly. Keep in mind that the quality of photo prints taken with the iPhone camera may not be as good as that of images captured using dedicated digital cameras, in part, because the iPhone camera does not have flash capabilities.

One way to copy photos from your iPhone to your computer is to run an import operation from a photo application, such as Adobe Photoshop Album 2.0 or later (PC), Adobe Photoshop Elements 3.0 (PC), or iPhoto 4.0.3 or later (Mac). For more details, see your program's help information.

① Connect your iPhone to your computer.

② Click **Start**.

③ Click **Computer**.

*Note: If you are using an earlier version of Windows, click **My Computer**.*

The Computer folder appears.

④ Double-click **Apple iPhone**.

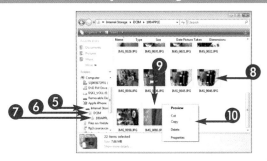

**5** Click **Internal Storage**.

**6** Click **DCIM**.

**7** Click **100APPLE**.

**8** Click to select the images you want to copy.

**9** Right-click a selected image.

**10** Click **Copy**.

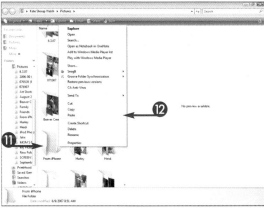

**11** Navigate to the folder into which you want to paste the images and then right-click it.

**12** Click **Paste**.

The images are copied to your computer.

**TIP**

**Try This!**

To select all of the images in the 100APPLE folder, press **Ctrl+A**. You can also press and hold down the **Shift** key as you click the first image and then the last image in the list. To select only certain images, hold down the **Ctrl** key as you click each image you want to copy.

# Surfing the Web with Your iPhone

If your iPhone has access to the Internet, either through a Wi-Fi network or the AT&T Edge network, you can use its built-in Safari Web browser to surf the Web.

If you have bookmarked favorite sites on your computer, you can transfer those bookmarks to your iPhone, allowing for easy access to all of your favorite pages. In addition, you can create new bookmarks using Safari on your iPhone. To help keep your bookmarks organized, the iPhone enables you to rearrange them, and to create folders in which you can group related bookmarks.

Of course, you are not limited to accessing pages that are bookmarked. You can display the intelligent keyboard in Safari and type any URL you choose.

Because the iPhone screen is smaller than a computer screen, Apple designed it to make it easy to zoom in on the information you need. You can also open multiple browser windows and switch back and forth between them. Safari's built-in search engine makes it easy to locate the pages you want.

If you are concerned about privacy and security, you can disable certain settings that may allow questionable content.

# Quick Tips

You have probably bookmarked, or flagged, Web sites that you visit regularly on your computer. (These sites are called Bookmarks in Safari and in some other browsers, and are called Favorites in Internet Explorer.) For example, you might have bookmarked a site you visit frequently to catch up on current events.

If you use the Safari Web browser (Mac or PC) or Internet Explorer (PC), you can copy your list of bookmarked sites to your iPhone during a sync operation. This enables you to access all your favorite sites quickly and easily using your iPhone.

After you sync your bookmarks to your iPhone, you can access them using the Safari Web browser, just as you would on your computer.

① Connect your iPhone to your computer.

② Click the iPhone entry in the iTunes Source list.

③ Click the **Info** tab.

④ Click **Sync bookmarks from** ( changes to ).

**Note:** You may need to scroll down to locate this check box.

⑤ Click the **Sync bookmarks from** and select the type of Web browser you use.

⑥ Click **Apply**.

iTunes copies the bookmarks to your iPhone.

The iPhone comes with the Safari Web browser, described by Apple as the most advanced Web browser ever used on a portable device. You can use it to explore the Internet just as you would use a Web browser on your Mac or PC.

To use Safari on your iPhone, you must be connected to the AT&T Edge network or to a Wi-Fi network. To determine whether you have access to a network, look for an Edge Network icon (a small E symbol) or a Wi-Fi icon along the top of the iPhone screen. If you are connected, you can launch your Web browser from the main iPhone screen.

**①** On the main iPhone screen, tap **Safari** (⊘).

Your iPhone launches the Safari Web browser, displaying the last-visited page.

You can easily direct the Safari Web browser to any Web site. One way is by selecting a bookmarked site. Another way is by typing the Web address, or URL, for a site into the browser window.

When you choose the second way, the iPhone displays its intelligent keyboard, which you can use to type in the address. The intelligent keyboard even has a special .com key, enabling you to conserve on keystrokes.

After you type a URL, if you decide you do not want to view the page, you can stop it from loading by tapping the Cancel Page Load button. You can reload a Web page by tapping the Refresh button. To return to recently viewed pages, tap the left- and right-arrow buttons.

① On the main iPhone screen, tap **Safari** (▨).

Your iPhone launches the Safari Web browser, displaying the last-visited page.

② Tap the address field at the top of the screen.

*Note: If the address field is not visible, tap the status bar along the top of the iPhone screen or scroll to the top of the page.*

The intelligent keyboard appears.

③ Tap  to clear the currently displayed Web address.

④ Type the URL for the page you want to visit.

*Note:* As you type, Safari lists Web sites that you have either bookmarked or visited recently containing the letters you have typed; you can choose from the list or keep typing.

⑤ Tap **Go**.

Safari displays the page you entered.

---

**Did You Know?**

If a Web page contains fields into which you must enter information, you can simply tap a field to invoke the intelligent keyboard and type the necessary information. To move to the next field, tap it, or tap the **Next** button. After you fill out all of the fields, tap the **Go** button or the **Search** button on the keyboard, or else tap the **Submit** link or button on the Web page.

You can bookmark favorite sites using the Safari browser, just as you can on your computer.

When you bookmark a Web site, you do not need to enter the URL in the address field to go to the site. Instead, you can display the list of all bookmarked sites and select the site from the list.

When you save a page as a bookmark, you can specify a title for the page, as well as the folder in which the bookmark for the site should reside. By default, bookmarks are saved in the top-level Bookmarks folder, but you can also save your bookmark in a subfolder. This enables you to group related bookmarks, making it easier to find the bookmark you want.

① With the page you want to bookmark open in Safari, tap ⊞.

The Add Bookmark screen appears.

② If you do not want to use the default name for the page, tap here and type your own name for the bookmark.

③ To select a different folder for the bookmark, tap ▶.

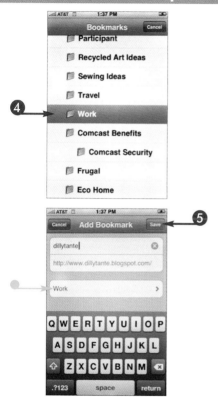

The Bookmarks screen appears.

④ Tap the folder in which you want to save the bookmark.

● The name of the folder you selected appears.

⑤ Tap **Save**.

The bookmark is saved.

**Apply It!**

Visiting a bookmarked page can be much easier than typing the page's Web address — especially if the Web address is long or difficult to remember. To visit a bookmarked site, tap the **Bookmark** button (📖). Then, in the Bookmarks screen that appears, tap the folder that contains the site, if necessary. Finally, tap the entry for the site to open it.

To help you keep your bookmarks organized, your iPhone enables you to edit the Bookmarks list. For example, you can group related bookmarks into folders. If none of the current folders applies to the site you want to bookmark, you can create a new folder. You can also change the order in which your bookmarks appear in the list, for example, placing bookmarks that you use most often at the top of the list.

If you no longer need or want a bookmark, you can delete it. This helps to keep your list of bookmarks concise and relevant. To delete a bookmark, tap the minus button next to its entry in the Bookmarks screen and tap the Delete button that appears.

① In the Bookmarks screen, tap **Edit**.

*Note:* To access the Bookmarks screen, tap **Bookmark ( ) in Safari.*

● To move a bookmark up or down in the list, tap ▤ on the right of the bookmark entry and drag the bookmark to its new location.

② To move a bookmark to a folder, tap the bookmark entry.

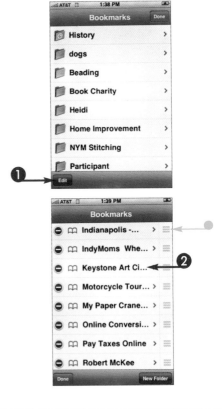

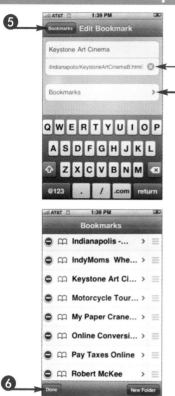

The Edit Bookmark screen appears.

- To change the bookmark's title, you can tap here, and then type the desired text in the field.

③ To select a different folder for the bookmark, tap >.

④ Tap the folder in which you want to save the bookmark.

Your iPhone returns you to the Edit Bookmark screen.

⑤ Tap **Bookmarks**.

Your iPhone returns you to the Bookmarks screen.

⑥ Tap **Done**.

**More Options!**

You can create a new folder in which to save a bookmark. Tap **Edit** in the Bookmarks screen, tap **New Folder**, and in the Edit Folder screen that appears, type a name for the folder. Tap **Bookmarks** to return to the Bookmarks screen, tap **Done** to confirm the creation of the new folder, tap the new folder in the list, and tap **Done** again in the screen that appears.

Although the screen of the iPhone is clear, it can be difficult to see the content on Web pages, especially print that appears too small.

To get a better look at a page, you can zoom in. One way to zoom in is to double-tap the part of the page you want to view up close. You can also reverse-pinch the page — starting with your thumb and index finger pinched

together, and then spreading them apart. For a wider view, you can turn the iPhone sideways.

You may also want to take a long view by zooming back out. To zoom out, you can double-tap the page again, or pinch the page, this time starting with your fingers spread apart and then pinching them together.

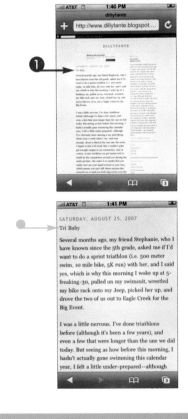

① Double-tap the spot on the Web page you want to view more closely.

● The contents of the page appear enlarged, showing the spot you tapped.

② To display a wide view of the content, rotate the iPhone 90 degrees to the left or right.

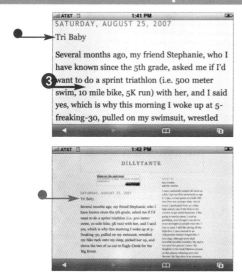

● The contents of the page shift to display in wide view.

*Note: To view the image vertically again, simply rotate the iPhone back to the vertical position.*

❸ To zoom back out, double-tap the screen.

● Your iPhone zooms out on the page.

**Did You Know?**

When you zoom in, if you can no longer see the portion of the page you want to view, you can pan around the page by dragging your finger over it. When you do, a scroll bar appears along the side or bottom of the screen, depending on whether you drag your finger horizontally or vertically, to help you determine which portion of the page is currently displayed.

In some cases, activating a link on a Web page automatically launches a new browser window. You can also launch new windows manually. For example, you might choose to display a site for booking airline tickets and a site for making hotel reservations at the same time, and then switch back and forth between the two as you make travel arrangements.

To switch from one open browser window to another, you can tap the Switch button, drag your finger across the screen to the left to cycle through the open windows, and then tap a window to view it in full-screen mode. To close a window, you can tap the Close button in the upper-right corner.

① To open a new browser window, tap **Pages** (□).

② Tap **New Page**.

**3** Tap the address field at the top of the screen.

The iPhone displays its intelligent keyboard.

**4** Type the URL for the page you want to visit.

**5** Tap **Go**.

Safari displays the Web page in a new window.

● The icon changes from 🔲 to 🔳, indicating the number of browser windows that are currently open.

**Did You Know?**

If you press and hold a link, its destination address appears next to your finger. You can also press and hold an image to determine whether a link is associated with it. A link can also open a map, dial a phone number, launch a new pre-addressed e-mail message, or play a media file. iPhone launches the necessary application to handle these types of links.

If you want to share the URL for a Web site with someone, you can e-mail it as a link from within Safari.

When you share a URL, your iPhone creates a new e-mail message containing the link, and displays its intelligent keyboard. You simply type the necessary contact information, a subject for your e-mail, and any message text you want to include.

If your iPhone is set up to use multiple e-mail accounts, the default one is used to send the Web link. If you want to use a different account, you must set it as the default account. For more information, see Chapter 5.

① In the Web page you want to share, tap the address field.

② Tap **Share**.

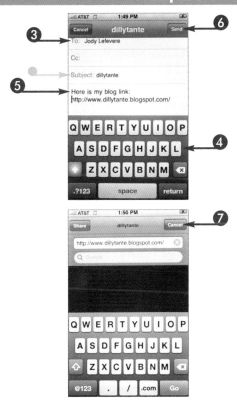

Your iPhone creates a new e-mail message containing a link to the page, and the intelligent keyboard appears.

③ Tap the **To** field.

④ Type the recipient's name or e-mail address.

● The Subject line contains the name of the page you are sending.

⑤ Tap here and type a message for the recipient.

⑥ Tap **Send**.

The iPhone sends your message and returns you to the screen containing the Share button.

⑦ Tap **Cancel** to return to the Web page.

**Attention!**

As you type the recipient's name or e-mail address in the To field, your iPhone displays a list of contacts that match what you type; tap the contact you want. You can also tap 🔵 to display the All Contacts screen, where you can select a contact. If the recipient is not in your Contacts list, you must type the addressee's e-mail address manually.

One way to search the Internet is to direct the Safari Web browser to the Google home page and then type your search criteria. An easier way to search the Internet is to use the built-in search function in Safari. This saves you the step of first directing the browser to a search engine's Web page; instead, you simply type your search criteria, and Safari automatically directs you to a search engine results page.

By default, Google is the search engine used by Safari, but you can change the search engine to Yahoo if you prefer.

① Tap the address field at the top of the Safari screen.

**Note:** *If the address field is not visible, tap the status bar along the top of the iPhone screen or scroll to the top of the page.*

The iPhone displays its intelligent keyboard.

② Tap the search field.

③ If necessary, clear any existing search criteria in the search field by tapping ⊗ to the right of the field.

④ Type the word or phrase for which you want to search.

⑤ Tap your search engine, for example, Google or Yahoo!.

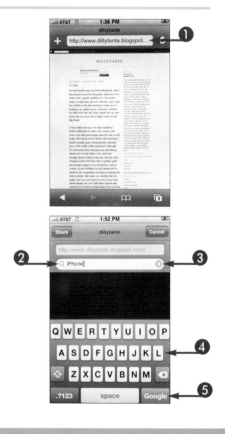

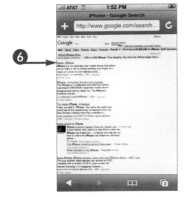

The results of your
search appear.

 **6** If an entry in the list
looks interesting, tap
its link.

The associated page
appears.

**TIP**

**More Options!**
Safari uses the Google search engine by default, but you can switch
the search engine to Yahoo! if you prefer. Tap the **Settings** button ([icon])
in the main iPhone screen, tap **Safari** in the Settings screen that
appears, tap **Search Engine**, and then tap the search engine you want
to set as the default. To confirm the setting and return to the main
iPhone screen, tap the **Home** button.

By default, Safari runs Web features that may compromise your privacy or security. For example, Safari allows the use of *plug-ins*, which enables the browser to display certain types of video content. Safari also allows for the use of JavaScript, which enables Web programmers to control certain page elements.

In addition, Safari accepts *cookies*, pieces of data that are copied to your computer or iPhone from a Web site. This enables that site to remember you the next time you visit, so that it can display personalized content or save you from having to enter personal information again.

You can change these default settings; however, some sites may not function correctly if cookies are disabled.

① Tap **Settings** (⚙) in the main iPhone screen.

The Settings screen appears.

② Tap **Safari**.

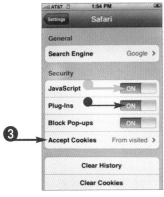

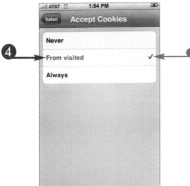

The Safari screen appears.

● To disable JavaScript, you can tap **ON** in the JavaScript entry to toggle it off.

● To disable plug-ins, you can tap **ON** in the Plug-Ins entry to toggle it off.

❸ Tap **Accept Cookies**.

❹ Specify whether you want to accept cookies by tapping an option.

● A check mark appears next to the option you chose.

❺ Press the **Home** button to confirm the settings and return to the main iPhone screen.

**More Options!**

Although Safari allows JavaScript, plug-ins, and cookies by default, it is set up to block *pop-ups* — those annoying new windows that open automatically, usually containing advertisements. However, this blocks only the pop-ups that appear when a page is closed or when you type the URL of a new page to open it. Pop-ups that open when you click a link are not blocked.

If you are conducting a job search, you might not want evidence of that search on your iPhone, especially if the iPhone is company-issued. To protect your privacy, you can clear your browser's History list.

You can also clear your cookies — those pieces of data that are copied to your iPhone from a Web site to enable that site to remember you the next time you visit.

Keep in mind that some sites may not function correctly if cookies are disabled.

Finally, you can clear the browser cache, which stores the content of pages you have viewed so that those pages will load more quickly the next time you visit them. You might clear the cache if the page you are visiting displays outdated content.

## CLEAR THE BROWSER HISTORY

① In the Safari Settings page, tap **Clear History**.

**Note:** To access this page, tap **Settings** (🔘) in the main iPhone screen, and tap **Safari** in the Settings screen that appears.

② Tap **Clear History** to confirm the operation.

Safari clears the History list.

## CLEAR COOKIES

① In the Safari Settings page, tap **Clear Cookies**.

*Note: To access this page, tap **Settings** (🔘) in the main iPhone screen, and tap **Safari** in the Settings screen that appears.*

② Tap **Clear Cookies** to confirm the operation.

Safari clears your cookies.

### Did You Know?

Another way to clear the History list is by first displaying it. To do this, open Safari and tap the **Bookmark** button (📖). In the Bookmarks screen, tap the **History** folder, and then tap **Clear**. Note that you can access any site displayed in this folder by tapping its entry in the list.

You can change Wi-Fi settings on your iPhone. For example, you can disable Wi-Fi connectivity if you prefer to use the AT&T Edge network, choose a different network, or log on to a network manually.

If your iPhone detects a Wi-Fi network that you have used before, it connects to it automatically. Otherwise, it displays a list of available networks from which you

can select. When you connect to a Wi-Fi network, a Wi-Fi icon appears along the top of the iPhone screen.

If there are not any Wi-Fi networks available, or if you choose not to connect to one, your iPhone connects to the Internet using the Edge network, and displays an Edge Network icon.

1 Tap **Settings** (⚙) in the main iPhone screen.

The Settings screen appears.

2 Tap **Wi-Fi**.

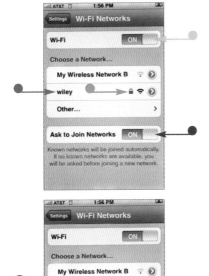

The Wi-Fi Networks screen appears.

● If Wi-Fi has been disabled, you can tap here to toggle it back on.

● You can specify whether you want the iPhone to prompt you to connect to unrecognized networks by tapping this option.

● Networks within your range appear here.

● A lock icon appears if a network requires a password.

③ Tap a network to connect to it.

*Note: If the network to which you want to connect is hidden, tap **Other** and enter the necessary information in the screen that appears, such as the name of the network and any security-related information.*

④ If prompted, type the necessary password.

iPhone connects to the network.

**Important!**

If you are on an airplane, you can use your iPhone to watch a movie or listen to music. However, due to air-traffic regulations, you must disable wireless connectivity during travel. To allow for this, the iPhone has a special airplane mode. To place your iPhone in airplane mode, tap the **Settings** button in the main iPhone screen, and tap **Off** next to Airplane Mode to toggle the feature on.

# Accessing Other Web Content with Your iPhone

You are not limited to using Safari to access Internet content on your iPhone. The device comes pre-configured with a few additional applications that allow access that is more direct to Web content. To use these applicationis, your iPhone must be connected to the Internet either through a Wi-Fi network or through the AT&T Edge network. If you are connected to a Wi-Fi network, a Wi-Fi icon will appear along the top of the iPhone screen. If you are connected to the Edge network, you will instead see an Edge Network icon. These applications include Stocks, Maps, and Weather.

The Stocks application enables you to quickly and easily check the performance of your favorite stocks, indexes, or funds, as well as research a company in whose stock, index, or fund you are interested. The Maps application allows you to view a map or satellite image of the location you specify, as well as obtain directions from the start and end point of your choice. You can use the Weather application to view a weather forecast for any location on Earth, as well as access general information about a location, such as a city guide, photos, and news articles.

# Quick Tips

If your iPhone is connected to the Internet, either through a Wi-Fi network or through the AT&T Edge network, you can use your iPhone to check the performance of your favorite stocks, indexes, or funds.

One way to do this is to launch the Safari Web browser and direct it to a financial Web site. However, a quicker approach is to use the iPhone Stocks application.

You can view activity over a period of one day, one week, one month, three months, six months, one year, or two years. You can also use Stocks to view general information about the company whose stock, index, or fund you are checking.

① Tap **Stocks** (📈) in the main iPhone screen.

② Tap the stock whose performance you want to see.

● The stock's current value appears here.

● The performance of the stock over a specific time span displays here.

③ To view the performance of the stock over a different time span, tap the time span you want to view.

● The stock's performance appears over the time span you chose.

This example changes the time span from 6 months to one day.

④ To view information about the company associated with the stock, tap **Yahoo** (Y!).

Your iPhone launches Safari, which displays a Web page containing information about the company associated with the stock.

**More Options!**

Yahoo! presents a Web page that shows you information about the company associated with the selected stock, index, or fund. This page includes links to the company Web site, stock information, links to newspaper articles about the company, information about the physical location of the company, and other related information.

By default, the Stocks application displays information about the following stocks: Apple, Google, Yahoo!, and AT&T. It also displays the Dow Jones Industrial Average (DJIA).

If you are not interested in tracking these stocks or the DJIA, you can delete them, and add new stocks of your own to track. You can also specify whether Stocks

should display financial information in numbers or percentages.

Stocks automatically updates financial information when you launch it. Keep in mind that there may be up to a 20-minute time lag between when a stock, index, or fund is updated on the market and when that update appears on your iPhone.

---

① In the Stocks screen, tap **Info** (ⓘ).

**Note:** *To access the Stocks screen, tap **Stocks** (▣) in the main iPhone screen.*

● You can use these buttons to switch between displaying information in numbers and percentages.

② Tap **Add** (➕).

The Add Stocks screen appears.

③ Type the name or the stock ID of the company whose stock you want to track.

④ Tap **Search**.

● Your iPhone displays a list of companies and stock symbols that match what you typed.

⑤ Tap the desired stock.

● The stock you chose is added to the list in the Stocks screen.

⑥ Tap **Done**.

### Remove It!

To delete a stock you no longer want to track, tap the **Add** button (🞢) in the Stocks screen. A list appears of the stocks you are tracking. Tap ⊖ next to the stock you want to delete, and then tap the **Delete** button that appears. When you are finished, tap the **Done** button.

Although the iPhone does not have GPS capabilities, it does feature a Maps application that enables you to view maps and satellite images of a location.

You can search for a location by typing an address, intersection, the name of a landmark, a Zip Code, or the name of a person in your iPhone contacts, if his or her contact entry contains an address. You can also view a map of a contact's location from within the contact's record by tapping the address in the record.

In addition to viewing a map of the location you enter, you can also view a satellite image of the location.

---

**①** Tap **Maps** (📍) in the main iPhone screen.

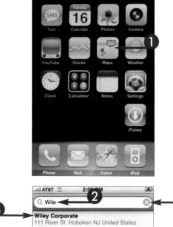

**②** Tap the **Search** field.

The iPhone intelligent keyboard appears.

**③** Tap **Delete** (⊗) to clear any existing search text.

**④** Type information about your location, such as a contact name.

**⑤** Tap **Search**.

Your iPhone displays a list of locations that match what you typed.

**⑥** Tap a location in the list.

● Your iPhone displays the location you specified.

⑦ To view a satellite image of the location, tap **Satellite**.

● Your iPhone displays a satellite view of the location.

***Note:*** *For a better look at a map or satellite image, you can "reverse pinch" or double-tap the map to zoom in. You can then pinch the screen to zoom back out. You can also drag your finger along the screen to reposition the map.*

### Did You Know?

To bookmark a location, tap the ⊳ next to the pushpin icon, tap **Add to Bookmarks**, type a name for the bookmark (or accept the default), and tap **Save**. To access the bookmarked location, tap the **Bookmark Maps** button (📖) next to the search field and, in the Bookmarks screen, choose a bookmark. To access recently viewed maps, tap **Recents** in the Bookmarks screen and tap the map you want to see.

You can use the iPhone Maps application to obtain directions to your destination, which you can view in either map or written form. Directions include a total distance and an estimated travel time. Depending on the region, you may also be able to view information about traffic levels along your route.

You can search for your start point and end point in different ways. For example,

you can enter an address, intersection, general area, landmark name, Zip Code, or the name of a person in your iPhone contacts, if his or her contact entry contains an address.

If you already have directions for a route, you can view them again by tapping the Bookmark Maps button next to a search field, tapping Recents, and tapping the directions search in the list.

①  With the Maps application open, tap **Get Directions** (⌘).

*Note:* To open the Maps application, tap **Maps** (⌘) in the main iPhone screen.

②  Tap the **Start** field.

③  Type the start location.

④  Tap the **End** field and type the end location.

*Note:* For help entering the location, see the section, "View Maps and Satellite Images."

●  To switch the start and end points, tap **Switch End Points** (⌘).

⑤  Tap **Route**.

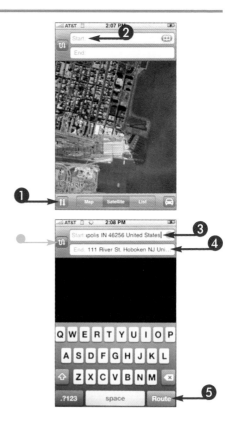

The route appears on a map.

**Note:** *To view traffic levels on highways along your route, tap the Car button (*  *). If data is available, red routes are moving at a rate of less than 25 mph; yellow routes are moving at 25 to 50 mph; and green routes are moving at over 50 mph.*

⑥ To switch to written directions, tap **List**.

The directions appear in written form.

**Did You Know?**

You can use Maps to locate a business. First, display a map for a general location, such as a city. Then enter a keyword for the type of business in the search field. The iPhone displays pushpin icons at locations that match the search; tap an icon to see the business name. To contact the business, tap its name. If a phone number is available, you can tap it to dial.

You can use the iPhone Weather application to view the current temperature along with a six-day weather forecast. This information is supplied by Yahoo! in partnership with The Weather Channel.

By default, the weather displays for Cupertino, which is the location of the Apple headquarters. Obviously, unless you live in Cupertino, you will want to view the weather in your own location. To add weather locations, see the section, "Add a New Weather Location." You can also delete locations.

If you have saved multiple locations, you can easily switch from one to the next. You can also view additional information about a location from within the Weather application, such as a city guide, an events guide, photos, and news articles.

① Tap **Weather** (📟) in the main iPhone screen.

The weather forecast displays for the last location you checked.

● These dots indicate how many locations you have saved in the Weather application.

② To view the weather at another of your saved locations, tap a dot or drag your finger across the iPhone screen.

The weather forecast appears for a different saved location.

③ To view additional information about this location, tap **Yahoo!** ().

Your iPhone launches Safari, which displays a Web page containing available information about the location.

---

**Did You Know?**

The weather display changes, depending on what time of day it is in the selected location. For example, if it is daytime, the display is light blue, and, if the location is experiencing clear conditions, a sun appears; if it is nighttime, then the weather display is dark purple, and, if the location is experiencing clear weather conditions, an image of a moon appears.

By default, the iPhone Weather application displays the weather for Cupertino, the location of the Apple headquarters. However, this information is of limited use if you do not live in Cupertino and have no immediate plans to visit.

Fortunately, you can add other locations to the Weather application. In addition to adding your home location, you can also add travel destinations, so that you can plan while you are on the go. If you have added a travel destination as a weather location, you can easily delete it after your trip is over.

The Weather application enables you to specify whether temperatures should appear in Celsius or Fahrenheit.

① With the Weather application open, tap **Info** (ⓘ).

**Note:** To open the Weather application, tap **Weather** (🌤) in the main iPhone screen.

The Weather screen appears.

⬤ You can tap here to switch from Fahrenheit to Celsius, or vice versa.

② Tap the **Add** button (➕).

The Add Location screen appears, displaying the iPhone intelligent keyboard.

③ Type the name of the city or town you want to add.

④ Tap **Search**.

A list appears of cities and towns whose names match what you typed.

⑤ Tap a location.

● The location is added to the Weather application.

⑥ Tap **Done**.

### Remove It!

To delete a location from the Weather application, tap the **Info** button (ⓘ), tap the ⊖ button next to the entry you want to remove, and tap the **Delete** button that appears. When you are finished, tap the **Done** button; the location is removed from the Weather application.

# Enjoying iPhone Extras

With your iPhone, you are not limited to surfing the Web, sending and receiving e-mail messages, talking on the phone, listening to music, watching video content, taking and sharing pictures, entering contact and calendar information, sending and receiving text messages, obtaining information about stocks and weather, and accessing maps, satellite images, and point-to-point driving directions.

You can also use the device for such practical purposes as setting an alarm and tracking the time across multiple time zones by adding clocks. Other features enable you to set a timer, which can also serve as a sleep timer that puts the iPhone to sleep after a specified time; use a stopwatch; calculate a tip or perform other simple math problems; and type notes to yourself, which you can then e-mail to others.

# Quick Tips

# Add a Clock

You can add multiple clocks to your iPhone using the Clock application. For example, if you frequently conduct business with people on the other side of the globe, or if you are on vacation in a different time zone, you can use the Clock application to set up a second clock for that geographic region, in addition to the clock you use at home.

In addition to adding new clocks, there may be times when you need to set the date and time of your main clock using the iPhone Settings options. For example, you may experience a problem with your battery, or the date and time recorded by the computer you use to sync your iPhone may be incorrect.

---

① Tap **Clock** (🕐) in the main iPhone screen.

② Tap **World Clock** (🌐).

Clocks that are set for your iPhone appear.

③ To add a new clock, tap ➕.

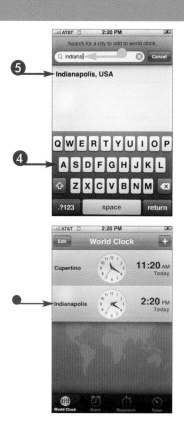

④ Using the intelligent keyboard that appears, type the desired location.

● As you type, the iPhone lists locations whose names contain the text you have entered.

⑤ Tap a location in the list.

● The clock appears for the location you selected.

**Remove It!**

To remove a clock, tap **Clock** (🕐) in the main iPhone screen, tap **World Clock**, tap **Edit**, tap ⊖ next to the clock you want to delete, tap the **Delete** button that appears, and then tap **Done**. To rearrange the clocks in the list, tap **Edit** in the World Clock screen, tap ☰ next to the clock you want to move, and drag up or down.

# Set an Alarm

You can set up your iPhone to sound an alarm at the time you specify. The alarm can be a one-time occurrence, or it can recur at the interval you choose. You can also set up the alarm to repeat; for example, if you need to wake up at a certain time each Tuesday, you can configure the alarm to sound each Tuesday at the time you specify.

To help you keep track of the alarms that you set, the iPhone enables you to label them with a descriptive name. The alarm can be configured to emit any one of the available ringtones. You can also set it up to support the Snooze function, which operates like the snooze functions found on most alarm clocks.

① Tap **Clock** (🕐) in the main iPhone screen.

② Tap **Alarm** (⏰).

The Alarm screen appears.

③ Tap ➕ to open the Add Alarm screen.

- To set a recurring alarm, tap **Repeat** and select the desired interval.

- To change the alarm sound, tap **Sound** and select the desired tone.

- To enable or disable the Snooze function, toggle this button.

④ Flick up or down to spin the hour, minute, and AM/PM portions of the wheel to the desired time.

⑤ Tap **Save** to set the alarm.

- When the alarm goes off, the iPhone plays the sound you chose and displays a notification.

⑥ Tap **OK** to turn off the alarm.

### Remove It!

To remove an alarm you have set from the list, tap the **Clock** button (🕐) in the main iPhone screen, tap the **Alarm** button, tap **Edit**, tap the ⊖ next to the alarm you want to remove, and tap the **Delete** button that appears. When you are finished, tap the **Done** button. The iPhone deletes the alarm.

# Use the iPhone Stopwatch

Many people use their iPhone to listen to music while exercising. To increase the usefulness of your iPhone, Apple has included a Stopwatch function to help you keep track of the duration of your workout (or for other purposes). If you are running on a track, you can use your iPhone Stopwatch feature to keep track of lap times. You can also use the stopwatch and listen to music at the same time.

In addition to providing a stopwatch, the iPhone also includes a timer. You can set up the timer to play a sound of your choosing when time is up; you can also set up the timer to shut off the iPhone after the set duration.

① Tap **Clock** (🕐) in the main iPhone screen.

② Tap **Stopwatch** (⏱).

The Stopwatch screen appears.

③ Tap **Start**.

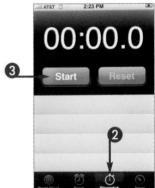

The timer begins.

**④** To record a lap time, tap **Lap**.

**⑤** Continue recording lap times as needed.

● Lap times are listed here.

**⑥** To stop the timer, tap **Stop**.

The timer stops.

**More Options!**

To use the iPhone timer, tap **Clocks** (🕐) in the main iPhone screen, tap **Timer**, and spin the hour and minute wheels as needed. To choose the sound that plays when time is up, tap **When Timer Ends** and choose a tone. You can also choose **Sleep iPod** to put the iPhone to sleep after the specified time, which is useful if you are listening to music while drifting off to sleep.

If you have a great idea while on the go, you can use your iPhone to type it using the Notes application.

When you launch the Notes application, a list appears of notes that you have written. When you create a new note, the iPhone intelligent keyboard appears. The date and time at which you created the note is added to it automatically.

After you type your note, you can view it at any time. Notes are sorted in the iPhone by date and time. If you have entered multiple notes, you can easily scroll through them. When you are finished with a note, you can delete it.

① Tap **Notes** (☐) in the main iPhone screen.

The Notes screen appears.

② Tap ➕.

The intelligent keyboard appears.

**3** Type your note.

**4** Tap **Done**.

The iPhone saves your note.

**Did You Know?**

If you want to e-mail a note to someone, you can easily do this by tapping the **E-mail** button (✉) at the bottom of the note. Your iPhone creates a new message. Type the recipient, edit the Subject line as needed, type any message text you want to include, and tap **Send**. For more information about working with e-mail messages, see Chapter 5.

After you type a note, you can view it at any time. Notes are sorted in the iPhone by date and time. They display in list form in the main Notes screen in the order in which you created them. Each entry in the list contains the date and time when you typed the note and the first few words in the note. To see the note in full, you must display it.

After you display a particular note, you can easily move to the next or previous note in the list. You can also e-mail a note.

When you are finished with a note, you can delete it. To delete a note, you tap the Delete button at the bottom of the screen.

① In the Notes screen, tap the note you want to view.

*Note: To display the Notes screen, tap Notes (□) in the main iPhone screen.*

The note appears.

● You can tap here to move to the previous note in the list.

● You can tap here to move to the next note in the list.

● You can tap **Notes** to return to the Notes screen.

If mathematics is not your strength, then you probably do not like figuring out how much to leave for a tip at the end of a meal, determining the price of a discounted item, and other similar mathematical tasks.

Fortunately, the iPhone includes a Calculator application that lets you

perform simple calculations. If you are looking to perform a complicated scientific or statistical calculation, this is not the tool for you. However, if you are attempting to, for example, balance your checkbook or calculate a library fine, then the iPhone Calculator application is the perfect tool.

① Tap **Calculator** (📟) in the main iPhone screen.

The iPhone Calculator screen appears.

② Tap the number and operator buttons to enter your equation.

③ Tap **Equal**.

Your iPhone displays the result.

# Index

# Index

# Index